PRAISE FOR *CHOICE & VOICE*

"Based upon sound reading theory and research, this is a practical book, written by teachers for teachers. Clearly understanding the relationship between student choice and student engagement, the authors fill their pages with suggestions about creating reading rich environments, integrating the various strands of the language arts, dealing with mandated curriculum, and structuring instructional time. Those of us distressed about those 'I hate reading' students will find this a tremendously useful book."—**Tom Scott, former director, English education, University of Wisconsin–Milwaukee**

"After reading this book, I am hopeful that teachers in all content areas will be convinced that they can and should craft a Collaborative Reading Workshop for their classes. The authors share tools, materials, research, and practical examples that can be easily adapted to any classroom while also showing the potential this approach has for building the reading, writing, and discussion skills of all students, regardless of ability. Just as important, Fleck and Heinemann illustrate how a Collaborative Reading Workshop builds a sense of community that fosters self-awareness, relational skills, empathy, and tolerance among students of diverse backgrounds, values, and interests. Try this approach and watch your students become empowered when they see that their voice matters and confident when they watch their literacy skills grow!"—**Marsha McCracken Voigt, coauthor,** *Disciplinary Literacy in Action*

"At a cultural moment in which many of us are looking for ways to 'spark joy,' *Choice & Voice* serves as a heartening reminder that the simple act of reading can provide the fulfillment, wonder, and human connection that we seek. In addition to offering practical resources such as discussion questions, sample assignments, and solutions to potential challenges both inside and outside the classroom, Fleck and Heinemann make an elegant, engaging argument for the way that reading strengthens the relationships between students, teachers, and communities. As soon as I finished reading *Choice & Voice*, I couldn't wait to pick up another book."—**Lindsay Starck, assistant professor, English, and codirector, MFA program, Augsburg University**

"The opportunities for self-selection and collaboration within a safe environment are true difference-makers for reluctant readers. I know this because I was one. If only an opportunity like Collaborative Reader Workshop existed for me as a young adult."—**Heath J. McFaul, associate principal, Barrington High School**

"For teachers who are curious about implementing more choice and independent reading, this book provides practical strategies for easing in productively. Its emphasis on building relationships among students, teachers, and the larger school community connects culturally relevant and responsive practices and addresses equity explicitly. As Fleck and Heinemann demonstrate, students in collaborative reader workshops develop habits of mind by setting goals, pursuing their passions, and increasing their appreciation for the diversity of texts and each other."—**Helen C. Gallagher, English division head, Oak Park and River Forest High School**

"As a college counselor, I often work with students who have not been prepared well enough to face the challenges college classes provide. From not feeling comfortable interacting with others in class to not being able to process what they read in their textbooks, many students struggle during their first term in postsecondary. Doing well at this level has more to do with self-management than it does with 'being smart.' *Choice & Voice* provides a structure for these students to practice and improve the social-emotional, critical-thinking, and goal-setting skills needed to be successful as a college student. Since Collaborative Reader Workshop works from a growth mindset perspective, it not only teaches students they are not limited, it provides them with the space to see and experience it for themselves."—**Matthew Cullen, counselor, Green River College**

"With its focus on building a community of engaged readers, *Choice & Voice* offers practical advice on achieving schoolwide buy-in for a program with proven success. The authors demonstrate ways to integrate authentic reading experiences into literacy curriculum with the ultimate aim of creating lifelong readers. Look no further for evidence that setting up a Collaborative Reader Workshop of your own is well worth the effort."—**Louise Brueggemann, librarian, Oak Park and River Forest High School**

"Structuring independent reading programs can be challenging for both new and experienced teachers alike. Collaborative Reader Workshop provides the 'what' and the 'why' for success. Offering a clear framework that empowers students to see themselves as literate, engaged learners, Fleck and Heinemann demystify the process that leads to lifelong reading."—**Donna L. Pasternak, professor, English education, University of Wisconsin–Milwaukee**

Choice & Voice

Choice & Voice

How to Champion Lifelong Literacy through Collaborative Reader Workshop

Stephanie Fleck
Jolene Heinemann

ROWMAN & LITTLEFIELD
Lanham • Boulder • New York • London

Published by Rowman & Littlefield
An imprint of The Rowman & Littlefield Publishing Group, Inc.
4501 Forbes Boulevard, Suite 200, Lanham, Maryland 20706
www.rowman.com

6 Tinworth Street, London, SE11 5AL, United Kingdom

Copyright © 2020 by Stephanie Fleck and Jolene Heinemann

All rights reserved. No part of this book may be reproduced in any form or by any electronic or mechanical means, including information storage and retrieval systems, without written permission from the publisher, except by a reviewer who may quote passages in a review.

British Library Cataloguing in Publication Information Available

Library of Congress Cataloging-in-Publication Data

Names: Fleck, Stephanie, 1987– author. | Heinemann, Jolene, 1989– author.
Title: Choice & voice : how to champion lifelong literacy through collaborative reader workshop / Stephanie Fleck, Jolene Heinemann.
Description: Lanham, Maryland : Rowman & Littlefield, 2020. | Includes bibliographical references and index. | Summary: "This book offers a clear model to help our readers establish a Reader Workshop in their classrooms."—Provided by publisher.
Identifiers: LCCN 2019059442 (print) | LCCN 2019059443 (ebook) | ISBN 9781475846485 (Cloth : acid-free paper) | ISBN 9781475846492 (Paperback : acid-free paper) | ISBN 9781475846508 (ePub)
Subjects: LCSH: Reading (Secondary) | Language arts (Secondary)
Classification: LCC LB1632 .F59 2020 (print) | LCC LB1632 (ebook) | DDC 428.4071/2—dc23
LC record available at https://lccn.loc.gov/2019059442
LC ebook record available at https://lccn.loc.gov/2019059443

Contents

Foreword   vii

Prologue   ix

Acknowledgments   xiii

Introduction: How to Use This Book   xv

PART I: THE WHAT

1. The Reading   3
2. The Writing   19
3. The Discussion   31
4. How to Confront Challenges   45
5. How to Make It Work for Your Students   61
6. How to Get Started Next Week   77

PART II: THE WHY

7. Academic Achievement   83
8. Social-Emotional Learning   95
9. Equity   107
10. Lifelong Reading Habits   115

Epilogue	123
Appendix: Book Lists	127
Works Cited	141
Index	143
About the Authors	149

Foreword

Reading and Writing Workshop, a powerful, student-centered approach to literacy within the context of authentic reading and writing, has been around for quite a while in elementary and middle school English language arts classes. It has been slow to show up in high school English classes, however, with some teachers citing daunting challenges:

- How will I make time for independent reading and still cover everything required by the standards?
- What if I am required by my department or district to teach specific whole-class texts and common writing assignments?
- Will kids actually read during independent reading time?
- Is it realistic to ask students to read a required text *and* another book?
- What if my principal thinks independent reading isn't rigorous enough?
- How can I ensure that students choose books at their grade levels?
- Does the focus on reading overshadow writing instruction?
- How will I assess workshop learning?

Fleck and Heinemann address each of these concerns, providing research regarding why the overall approach works as well as compelling arguments for the effectiveness of their collaborative model. I believe they nail it when they say, "Sure, it might be easier for English teachers to tell their students what and how to think, but students learn best when they have a chance to think about a text on their own terms first." This understanding is at the core of workshop teaching.

But although the idea may sound good, what exactly does that look like in a secondary classroom? Once you begin reading, it becomes clear. And if you need quick, concrete suggestions, flip to the boxes and tables in each chapter where you'll find book talk themes, quick-write prompts, rubrics, options for structuring reading time, and, best of all, bulleted, sequential steps outlining the plan on which this book is based: Collaborative Reader Workshop. The authors describe a unique way of incorporating the workshop approach into a more traditional curriculum, with a major bonus called collaborative discussion.

Maybe it's because Fleck and Heinemann are in the classroom working every day with students and facing the inevitable challenges that come with workshop teaching that they have been able to design a way to fit such a model into a conventional English curriculum. I suspect it's more than that, however. I think it's because these teachers, even as they worked really hard to ensure that they were covering the skills in the curriculum, felt that their students were missing important opportunities to engage in real-world reading, writing, and dialogue. As they say in their book, they wanted more—they wanted their students to become well-rounded, thoughtful people who felt part of a community, confident in their abilities to interact with others regarding important ideas. What's more, they wanted their students to experience the many advantages that frequent and wide reading provides. They found a way to do that and more.

If you're not sure that you are ready to make the leap into what Fleck and Heinemann acknowledge can be a "messy" process, take it a step at a time. Through this book, experienced workshop teachers can add to their repertoire, and teachers new to the model can feel supported as they give it a try. In any case, transitioning to a workshop model such as the one Fleck and Heinemann suggest will provide academic, social, and intrinsic rewards that will last far longer than the next lesson on a curriculum map or a textbook table of contents.

—ReLeah Cossett Lent

ReLeah Cossett Lent is the author of *Overcoming Textbook Fatigue: 21st Century Tools to Revitalize Teaching and Learning* (2012), *This Is Disciplinary Literacy: Reading, Writing, Thinking, and Doing . . . Content Area by Content Area* (2016), and *Disciplinary Literacy in Action: How to Create and Sustain a School-Wide Culture of Deep Reading, Writing and Thinking* (2019).

Prologue

*I hate books.
I don't read.
Books are boring.*

These words hurt. Every time a student speaks them, we—along with many other teachers we know—react viscerally.

Then we perk up and tell our bored students that reading is good for them, that reading will make them better students, that they should just try a few more pages, and that they haven't found the right story yet.

But simply rebutting these statements isn't enough. It might be enough to encourage students to keep their opinions to themselves, but it's not enough to change how that student *feels* about reading. This idea—that we want to change the way our students *feel* about reading—was the first step toward Collaborative Reader Workshop.

We are storytellers. All of us. From birth to death, we absorb the details around us, tell our own stories, and talk about other people's stories. So how do our students—who are full of stories, who enjoy movies and video games with exciting storylines, who love to exchange stories with their friends and family—transform from storytellers (and story lovers!) outside of school to people who say things like "I hate reading" in the classroom?

It's not as if we're trying to bore our students. When we assign a novel to the class, we pick books we think our students will love. We usually pick books that we, ourselves, love: *The Great Gatsby*, *The Crucible*, *Devil in the White City*. These books are considered canon for a reason: the prose is poetic and beautiful, the characters are complicated and tragic and so *real*, the plots—love triangles and lies and deceit and murder!—are instructive and compelling. There's so much to analyze! There's so much to talk about! There's so much to love!

Unfortunately, our students don't always agree. How many times have you heard students say they never actually read a book in any English class? How many times, after you mention a major plot point in class, has a student yelled out, "Wait! That happened?!" You can only sigh because those pages were assigned four days ago. How often is it clear that a student skimmed enough of a book to finish an assignment but not enough to engage in a conversation about the rest of the story?

Let's face it: most students can make it through an English class without ever reading a novel. If they don't enjoy reading, they find ways not to read. With that in mind, we tried to think about what we, as readers, enjoy about reading. Sure, we read for professional development courses, and we read to learn best practices in our field, and we certainly read countless student essays. So, yes, we do some type of reading every day. And much like our students, we do much of this reading—as interesting and important as it may be—because we *have* to.

But what kind of reading do we *enjoy*? What kind of reading keeps us up at night? What kind of reading do we want to bring to our students?

Used books in a coffee shop, audiobooks on the train, book talks over dinner, heated debates about how a book compared to the movie, the news that our sister, who was never a big reader, already finished a book we recommended because she couldn't put it down—this is the kind of reading we love. This is the kind of reading we *need* in order to be better people and to lead better lives. And this is the kind of reading we want to bring to our classroom.

We can't bring a coffee shop to class. We can't bring our friends and loved ones either. But we can build a community of readers. We can give our students choice about what they read and time to read whatever it is that they chose. We can help them to experience reading outside of the context of an upcoming essay or unit exam. We can show them that *we* read for enjoyment all the time and that other adults—their science teachers, their deans, the school tech guys—read for enjoyment, too. We can give them time to talk about reading they do enjoy—whether it's a book they're reading right now or something they remember reading and loving years ago—on a regular basis with people within and outside the classroom. We can give them time to find the right book for them, as well as permission to break up with a book when things aren't going well.

All of this comes together in Collaborative Reader Workshop. Every day, our students read, and once a month (for us, it's on first Fridays) we invite other teachers and staff members that students run into all over the school into our rooms to facilitate small book club–style discussions about whatever it is everyone is choosing to read.

Because students are reading different books, each month has a focus, and our students have prepared for the discussion. Then they reflect on how the discussion went, how it's going with their book, and what they might want to read next. We put up string lights to set the mood. Sometimes we bring snacks.

But the most important thing we do is this: we stop making reading all about work. In our classrooms, we don't read because of standards or administrative demands or parent concerns or grades or test scores or societal pressure.

Instead, reading is about the simple things we want (and need) as readers and as human beings: connections with others, discussions that go in different directions, and excitement about telling our own stories and sharing our insights about others. Not only is this the foundation of Collaborative Reader Workshop, it's also the foundation of our lives as readers both inside and outside of the classroom.

If you're reading this book, odds are that these are your foundational, soul-shifting reasons for reading, too. And we're hoping to give you a way to pass on these reasons for reading to all of your present and future students.

This book gets you started.

Collaborative Reader Workshop is accessible for any middle grade or secondary classroom regardless of tracking restrictions. Throughout this book, we provide clear guidelines, practical adaptations, and usable resources. This book also gives you the know-how and confidence to explain the importance of self-selected, independent reading and reader workshop to your administration. More than anything, though, we hope this book leaves you feeling (re)invigorated about the teaching of literacy and exhilarated about bringing love into your students' reading lives.

Acknowledgments

Many people contributed their time and energy to helping us develop this book. We would like to thank our readers—Will Ejzak, Rob Baker, Clarissa Greguska, Raquel McGee, Moira Quealy, Gisele Ramilo, Elizabeth Rohner, and Shannon Wojciechowski—for their thoughtful commentary. Thank you, too, to ReLeah Lent for offering advice to support our first foray into publishing and for graciously writing the foreword to this text.

We also want to thank those educators who have consistently participated in Collaborative Reader Workshop, helping us to create a community of readers at both high schools. Thank you to Janet Anderson, Kevin Art, Rob Baker, Louise Brueggemann, Kathleen Duffy, Erika Eckart, Doug Hill, Ninja Idrizi, Sarah Kirkorsky, Jessie Meyers, Laura Minerva, Joe Molloy, Moira Quealy, Meghan Sclafani, Gisele Ramilo, Jennifer Robinson, Bill Rohner, Dave Udchik, Jen Walsh, and Cary Waxler for your consistent and enthusiastic support. And we need to make a special shout-out to Jen Walsh for contributing to our Collaborative Reader Workshop presentation at the National Council of Teachers of English convention in 2017.

We would be remiss if we did not acknowledge the reader workshop greats who have inspired our practice: Nancie Atwell, Kelly Gallagher, and Penny Kittle. We would also like to thank all of the authors our students continue to love and offer our deepest gratitude to two in particular who continue to connect with our students (and their teachers) through writing and social media: Andrew Smith and Robin Benway.

Finally, thank you to our partners, Paul and Will, for putting up with us as this book took over part of our lives. Thank you to our parents, Bob and Monica Heinemann and Irwin and Mindy Weiss, for nurturing our own reading lives. And thank you to Aubrey Fleck for being a lovable distraction and future Collaborative Reader Workshop participant.

Introduction

How to Use This Book

Between the two of us, we've read a lot of pedagogy books. Some were more useful than others. With that in mind, we have divided this book into two parts: "The What" and "The Why."

In part I, we tell you what Collaborative Reader Workshop is, how it looks on a day-to-day basis, and how you can set it up in your classroom. If you already believe in the power of self-selected, independent reading and collaborative discussions, that might be all you need. But if you or your administration still has questions about whether Collaborative Reader Workshop is worth the time, part II is for you. In this section, we dive into the research to explain the theory behind the madness: how Collaborative Reader Workshop creates higher-achieving students—and better people.

Part I

THE WHAT

Chapter One

The Reading

> I've had many struggles throughout my reading journey. . . . I've hated reading for many years. I disliked having to read certain books by force. But once I had the chance to read books I liked, things changed for me.—
> Leslye, high school student

Ever had a student say "I'll watch the movie" when studying a class text? Or upon the mere sight of a book, proclaim loudly "I hate reading!" to the entire room?

It's a sad truth: adolescents aren't reading as much as they used to. Not only do they lack time during school—on average, only 2 percent of time in a high school classroom is spent on reading (Goodlad 2004, 107)—but most students aren't reading outside of school, either. The National Endowment for the Arts (NEA) (2007) found that high school students spend only seven to ten minutes per day on voluntary reading (2) and that, as a result of all this time spent *not* reading, only a third of high school seniors read at a proficient level (13).

If your students are not reading in your classroom, it's a pretty sure bet they're not developing healthy reading habits outside of it, either. This is why Collaborative Reader Workshop sets aside class time for students to read *every day*. Giving young readers time to read what they want to read every day allows them to develop their literacy skills while learning to understand their own interests, preferences, and reading habits.

Chapter 1 details this first element of Collaborative Reader Workshop: self-selected, independent reading. It shows how to set up daily reading time and encourage your students to participate.

SELF-SELECTED, INDEPENDENT READING

The words "independent reading" make most high school students cringe (literally, figuratively, or both). And it makes sense: they're practically adults. They will read if and when they want to.

But here's the thing: even if they want to read, they don't. It's been documented again and again: Nearly half of young adults, ages eighteen through twenty-four, read *no* books for fun (NEA 2007). And the most recent surveys show that it's only getting worse over time (NEA 2018).

If you're reading this book, you think this is a problem. Maybe you've asked your students and received these common responses:

- I used to read, but now I don't have time.
- I have too much homework.
- I get home from sports practice or club meetings or my part-time job too late.
- Reading is boring.

That last one is key: Many students don't realize that reading is something they'd like to do. They haven't found a book that speaks to them, a book they can see themselves in. School has given them a chance to read novels from the canon but not books they can see their own stories in, not books they love.

Give them that chance. This is the most important work an English teacher can do. Call it whatever you want and structure it however you want, but give them the chance to find and read the books they love. Help them to associate reading with relaxation and enjoyment, an escape from the hectic school day.

Create Time for Reading

In its November 2019 "Statement on Independent Reading," the National Council of Teachers of English (NCTE) is adamant that English language arts teachers provide "intentional, protected time" for independent reading in the classroom. Since volume matters—students who read more become better readers—teachers need to guard this time, saving it from being swallowed up by other academic and administrative concerns.

Sounds great, right? But how do you fit it in? Every school schedule is different, but don't worry. You have options.

One idea is to schedule a short amount of daily reading time, whether it be ten or fifteen minutes, that allows students to read a little bit each day. If the thought of fitting this in every day is overwhelming, you could also schedule independent reading twice a week, giving them more time in each sitting.

The Reading

Table 1.1. Options to Structure Reading Time

Strategy	Pros	Cons
Daily reading (10 to 15 minutes)	• Creates daily routine • Short amount of time, easier to sustain for struggling readers • Easy to add time if a day is missed. Just read twenty minutes the next class period	• Short amount of time, harder for avid readers or students reading challenging texts • Can be hard to do daily, depending on class schedule or curriculum (block schedule)
Twice per week (20 to 25 minutes)	• Can allow for a more flexible schedule • Creates weekly routine • Allows flexibility: can be different amounts of time or same amount each day ranging from ten minutes to an entire class period	• Students won't be reading every day • Can feel inconsistent (e.g., if Monday is a reading day, you'll have to be flexible with the schedule when it comes to holidays)
Once per week (entire class period)	• Allows for a longer period of reading time • Consistent routine (same day each week) • Easier planning for that class period/day	• Students won't be reading every day • Longer period of time can be difficult for reluctant or struggling readers • Takes up a large chunk of class time at once, which can be tricky if students are working on a project

This may be the best option for schools that have department-mandated curriculum. Alternatively, you could also choose one day a week and give students a full class period to read. This allows extended reading time and a consistent routine without cutting into your daily class time. See table 1.1 for a breakdown of the pros and cons for each option.

There are no hard and fast rules about how to give students time to read. Do what works for you and adjust as you go. It's possible that what works wonderfully one year won't work at all the next. No system is perfect, but perfect or not, a system that allows your students time to read will have an impact on each student as an individual and as a lifelong reader.

Once you choose your reading structure, you have two jobs: to show your students that you, too, value reading and to help them stay focused and engaged. It's incredibly easy to think of daily independent reading time as time to catch up on grading or emails. Keep in mind that students think this way, too. If you don't model healthy reading habits, it's easy for them to see time for reading as time to catch up on math homework for next period or to text a friend in another class.

It's not uncommon for a reluctant reader to get really excited about a book right after you book-talk it, only to start staring off into space after about ten pages when the novel's plot isn't immediately gripping. While your students read, quietly conference with them. Start with the ones who clearly aren't into their books. Ask what's going on. Maybe they're distracted by their phones. Maybe they have a question about the plot. Maybe they're simply at a slow part of the book but trust it will pick up later. When you see the telltale signs—phones out, eyes glazed over, science homework next to the book—find out what's going on. It's not effective for a teacher to "drop everything and read" if that makes it easier for the student to fake read.

When you aren't conferencing with students, you should be reading, too. If you want students to value this time, show them that you value it, too, by reading a book of your own choice, purely for pleasure. When reading time ends, talk with your students about your own reading. Tell them how insane the scene you just read was. Tell them what's going on with your characters and ask what's going on with theirs. These moments are brief, but they allow students to see you as a reader, someone who practices what she preaches. You're engaging them in discussion about your book and theirs while modeling the excitement that the right book can bring to their lives. If you're not familiar with young adult (YA) literature, this is a good time to get acquainted. By choosing to read books your students love, you're showing them that you value a variety of genres. You're showing them that English teachers love *Romeo and Juliet* and *Perfect Chemistry* alike because they're both excellent stories, a fact that you can gently remind them when it comes time to read canonical texts: it's a good story just like that YA book you love! Give it a try!

And if you already love YA books, give another genre a try. Get out of your comfort zone and let the students know that's what you're doing. The more you are willing to take risks and try new things, the more they are willing to do the same, not because you told them to, but because you showed them how valuable it can be.

Create a Classroom Library

In *Readicide* (2008), Kelly Gallagher identifies "the single most important thing" he had done in his teaching career: filling his classroom with books. If you want your students to find stories they love, surround them with books. If you are lucky enough to have your own classroom—or to share a classroom with another educator who values in-class reading—build a classroom library in easily accessible spots throughout the room. Empty bookshelf? Fill it up! No bookshelves? Line a counter or table with choices. No counter space? Line the floors along the wall.

According to the 2005 National Assessment of Education Progress Report (Miller 2014, 80), classroom libraries matter. When students enter an English class full of books, they are more likely to spend time reading, think more positively about reading, and demonstrate higher levels of reading proficiency.

And it makes sense. If students are in a room where books are not readily available (or a teacher isn't readily available to slip a few personalized suggestions on their desk), why would they think about reading? They have digital devices and other students surrounding them, so if they don't see books being used, read, and displayed, there's no reason to even think about them. When students forget their books at home, they can try out a few books from the class library. When a student finishes a book, another one is only steps away. It's a little like Netflix's business model: if you provide enough choices, they'll likely want to watch something.

Put some thought into how you design the space. If you have enough books, you can organize them into fun, student friendly categories (think about your favorite Barnes & Noble table displays). "Tough Stuff" might include books that deal with trauma, addiction, and loss; "Love You Like a Love Song" for love stories; and "Are You Afraid of the Dark?" for horror. You can find tons of printable, premade genre labels online. Not enough books to create separate categories? Stack them according to author last name to make them easy to find or line them up by color for a rainbow effect.

But where do the books come from? Once you start looking, you will find ways to stock your library through donations, grants, and book sales. Maybe your library begins with only a few stories. That's a start! Over the years, it will grow. Meanwhile, those twenty books will show students that reading is important to you.

But what if you don't have a physical space? If you teach in a school with more students than classroom space, you may share many different classrooms, moving among them throughout the day. This puts an additional burden on you: now you have two or three or four classrooms to fill with books.

This is a time to go digital. If your books are in one room, create a digital library to show students in your other classes what's available. Google Sites is free and accessible, especially if your school uses the Google Suite already, but there are many free website designers out there.

Just like you would in a physical space, you can create a digital organization with snappy, student friendly shelf titles like "Books for the Beach" and "OMG. Drama" to help students navigate the choices on the digital platform. One huge perk of a digital library is that you can include links to help students

HOW TO BUILD A CLASSROOM LIBRARY

School and local libraries—Ask your librarians! In the current digital age, many libraries are condensing their print copies as they transition toward more digital copies. They often give away books to make space for new ones. Inquire about any books they don't need anymore and whether they'd be willing to donate to your classroom.

Parents and students—Go straight to the source and let your students and their parents and families know that you're building your classroom library and would love any contributions they have. Gallagher (2009) suggests asking graduating seniors to donate a favorite book to "leave a literary footprint" (53). Parent donations can lead to new floor lamps, plants, and shelving donations, too!

Grants—Your school, state, or community might offer grants to teachers for specific projects. Let them know that you are building a classroom library. Oftentimes, they love giving money for you to buy books for your students!

GoFundMe—Online crowdsourcing is another way to fundraise for books. Make sure to share your fundraiser through social media.

Home shelf—Go through your own book collection—ask family, friends, and neighbors, too—to see if you have books you loved but don't need anymore. Do the same with magazines. Clearing room on your own shelves give you an excuse to refresh your home library, too!

Used book sales—Your local resale shop likely has tons of bestsellers for low prices. Goodwill and Salvation Army, for example, price used books from $2.99 for the most popular books to 99 cents for paperbacks.

Authors—Keep in touch with authors via social media. Sometimes they'll send free copies of books your way. They may announce giveaways or drawings for books or magazine subscriptions. You can always reach out to them via snail mail, too, letting them know your students love their books and asking if they have any they could donate.

research what books are about on Goodreads, Amazon, Barnes & Noble, and so forth. Students can navigate these links to easily check out a book's cover art, read reviews, or even preview the first couple pages.

A digital library allows all students, regardless of what classroom they're in, to explore their options and then find them in their classroom, school, or local library. If you want to make your classroom library more accessible, create a book request form through Google Forms so you can track which books students are interested in. Then bring their book selections to class the next day.

It can be tricky to share books and track which students are reading books. You can set up a digital checkout system, create an index card system, or simply use a sheet of paper on a clipboard. Sometimes you will lose books (even after begging students to remember to bring them back), but the fact that you have given your students easy access to a variety of choices is what allows them to become readers. According to NCTE (2019), choice is essential if teachers want to "motivate, engage, and reach a wide variety of readers."

So it's worth losing a book now and then. Think of this way: if a book is "stolen" from the classroom, that means a student loved it enough that they took it home to read. Maybe they forgot to bring it back, but maybe they didn't want to part with it. So it's working! Immersing your students in a world of reading is the most important work you can do.

> **TEACHER TIP: MOIRA'S BOOK LOVE LIBRARY**
>
> For Moira Quealy, an English teacher at Barrington High School, a lost book is a chance to celebrate the stories her students love: "The price of taking a book home from my classroom is an index card telling me what they like about the book. It makes my heart happy to read them later."

Create a Cozy Reading Space

If you have your own classroom, make the space cozy. If your classroom has windows, keep the overhead lights off and allow the students to read in natural sunlight or with low lighting from lamps and string lights. Bring in a rug or comfy chairs. Allow students to sit on the floor against the wall or on a window ledge. Provide easy storage for students to keep the books they've checked out.

On the walls, celebrate reading with artwork. When a student finishes a book, ask him or her to design a book spine on a rectangular piece of paper and start building a visual bookshelf of all the books students have read throughout the year. Or print out the cover art of the books your students have finished reading and display those on a bulletin board. Visual reminders of your students' literacy successes build an environment that encourages them to keep reading.

If you teach in multiple classrooms, it's still possible to set the positive vibe for reading. A cozy reading space can mean sitting on desks, curling up in the nook by the door, stretching out on a counter, or simply stretching legs out on a chair in front of them. Modeling this is especially important; as students see you making use of multiple areas in the room, they will be encouraged to do the same.

Music is another way to set a mood. Free platforms like Spotify offer a variety of "focus" playlists comprised of orchestral, instrumental, or atmospheric pieces, or you can create your own playlist as a class. Students can even follow this playlist on their own devices to continue listening at home. If the class has voted on playing quiet music during reading time, but one or two students prefer silence, let them read in the hallway. And if they're comfortable sitting at their desks with headphones on to read? Let them.

Choice is key. Allow choice not only in the books they read but in the spaces they inhabit while reading. Knowing that their teacher cares about their comfort as a person and a reader does wonders for opening students up to reading. Allowing them ownership of the classroom space helps them to feel ownership over their reading.

This is the core of what daily independent reading is about: making it their space, their time, and their choice. Then jumping in with them. Daily independent reading might be one of the only breaks in their day during which they have this kind of agency over their decisions. And helping their brains to associate that feeling of freedom with the idea of reading? No textbook or whole-class read has that kind of magic.

BOOK TALKS

Now that you are committed to giving your students time to read in class, don't set them loose without guidance. Finding a book probably feels like second nature to you: you skim the shelf, pick one up whose title or cover art appeals to you, and read the back cover to see if you're interested. But many adolescent readers have no experience with this practice; they don't know where to start. And that's where the book talk comes in.

It's helpful to think of a book talk like a movie trailer: you highlight the best parts of the story to make your audience want to experience the whole thing. In fact, book trailers are a thing all over the internet, created by authors, publishers, students, and book lovers to promote books to a wider audience. Although book talks (and book trailers) are an art form in and of themselves, their most important function in Collaborative Reader Workshop is to connect the various readers in your classroom with options for daily independent reading.

Book talks can be shared daily, weekly, or even less frequently. The frequency of book talks can be adjusted to align with the interests of your students. Freshmen in advanced honors English, for example, tend to love book talks, but many of them are also avid readers before they enter the classroom. If they were asked to view a book trailer on their own or had access to a slideshow of book suggestions from the school librarians, they would probably give themselves book talks every day.

However, although many students in advanced classes know there are books that they *need* to read—for English or psychology or even for SAT preparation—they're doing this reading for the points and what the points mean for their college applications. For these students, daily book talks may be the catalyst they need to see reading not only as a step toward their future but also as a habit that brings joy and mindfulness to a stressful school day.

This isn't always the case for students in average college prep courses. Many of these students say that they hate reading or, even if they used to read, have not found a story they've enjoyed for years. Of course, many of them feel this way about anything school related, so giving them resources to find books independently would not work for most of them.

Knowing this, it's effective to integrate book talks into all of your classes, regardless of level, at some point during the day, week, month, or even semester. Setting aside time (whatever amount works for you) for book suggestions offers students myriad options, genres, and voices, showing them that books, like classrooms, are full of diverse stories.

THE RULES OF BOOK TALK

1. *No Talking about Book Talk*
   This is a joke. It's a reference to *Fight Club*, which is a great book to book talk. Deliver this line to your students as you see fit.
2. *No Digital Distractions*
   That means phones, computers, iPads, and whatever else the tech industry has created by the time you read this.
3. *No Other Kinds of Distractions*
   This clarifies that students can get distracted even if they're not holding a phone. This includes (but is not limited to) walking into the room late, leaving the room to use the bathroom, eating chips, drinking from a plastic water bottle, throwing things across the room to the trash can, throwing things across the room at other people, asking questions about prom, and so forth.
4. *No Talking while the Speaker Is Talking*
   Often, when asked these rules, students rename this one "Shut the Hell Up."
5. *Yes, Active Listening!*
   Adapt this as needed. Some suggestions: Students should look at the reader. They should raise their hands if the speaker asks a question or nod if the speaker says something they agree with. Basically, they shouldn't have their heads on their desks. (Again, when you review the rules of book talk, they may remember this as "Shut the [Insert inappropriate and slightly aggressive word here] Up." Whatever gets through to them, right?)

The Structure of Book Talks

The biggest key to a successful book talk is to talk about a book you love. That said, the general components of a book talk are as follows:

1. Identify the book's title and author
2. Summarize the basic conflict and plot points (without giving away too much)
3. Share how you found this book and/or what you love about it
4. Read a short excerpt to get your audience interested
5. Listen to the wild applause

It's best to have a copy of the book with you so you can hold it up and show the students the cover and the white space on the pages. If a student is especially interested in a book, you can put it in his hands right then and there so he can try it out during independent reading.

But if you read a library copy of the book and had to return it, no worries! If you don't have a copy in your classroom library, make a slide to show the cover art or pull it up with a quick Google search. The same goes for excerpts. If you don't have the book in front of you, it's easy to find quotes on sites like Goodreads and Google Books.

It's best to start the year with high-interest books. (Check out the appendix for a list of student favorites.) But since you want your students to experience a wide and varied reading life, challenge yourself to read and share new genres.

Mix it up: give them screenplays, nonfiction, and short stories. Use throwback Thursdays, commonly referred to as #TBT on social media, to talk about books written in or about past decades. Show them a bit of yourself at their age with a week of books that you loved in high school. If you usually share the young adult love stories you enjoy, set aside a week for graphic novels or science fiction or sports stories. Even if a genre isn't your cup of tea, you never know what will spark interest in that reluctant reader. Table 1.2 includes ideas for themed weeks.

If you give engaging book talks full of variety, intrigue, and cliffhangers, students will react with enthusiasm, but even if you've built a classroom library, you won't have enough copies of every book for every student. So encourage students to keep track of the books they want to read next.

Some teachers simply ask students to create a "Want to Read" list on the inside cover of their English notebooks, but you may want to create a more official form for students to keep ready or invite students to keep track of books on Goodreads, a social media site for readers. You can also help them to keep track by posting a list of book talks on your school's learning management system or on a bulletin board in your classroom. These systems become

Table 1.2. Book Talk Theme Week Possibilities

Theme	What It Entails
Guest speaker week	Survey the students, contact those you know in the building/community, and bring in as many guest "book talkers" as you can!
Book trailer week	Find good book trailers to show in place of a book talk each day. You will need to introduce the book briefly beforehand, and some trailers need a bit of extra explanation afterward.
Throwback week	This week, every day is a classic book. For most students, classic can mean anything from Victorian England up through the early 2000s. Decide what works for your kids. Alternatively, give a throwback Thursdays (#TBT) book talk once a week.
Teacher favorites	This is a fun one because students get to know you through the books you love. You can do your personal favorites now, your favorites from when you were your students' age, or both!
Movie week	This allows you to talk to students about books that are also movies. There are tons of current options on Netflix, but you can also do older texts like *Jurassic Park*, which many of the students know as a movie but not as a book. Choose books that allow you to emphasize the differences between the mediums and encourage students to explore both texts so that you can talk to them about the differences.
Banned books week	Combine this with whatever banned books week activities your school or library may be planning. Explain what the week is, why books get banned, and book-talk all the banned books you can! Make sure to point out why they got banned (because we all know if you tell teenagers *not* to do something . . .).
Genre week	You can do this with a variety of genres from nonfiction to fiction or from comedy to celebrity biographies. Screenplays and teleplays are fun, underutilized texts as well. Get as creative as you wish! This also helps students (and teachers!) who are used to one genre learn about options outside of their comfort zone.

a resource for students to remember which stood out to them, so they always know what to read next.

The Book Talk Speakers

Although it's important that your students know that you love books, you also want them to know that adults outside of the English department read, too. Invite staff from around the building to give book talks during a guest speaker week. Students love to discover that their wrestling coach listens to audiobooks while he works out or to hear their dean swear aloud while reading an excerpt from *Carter Finally Gets It*. Guest speakers expose students to a greater variety of books while building a culture of literacy in the school. Table 1.3 shows how you can make use of different kinds of book talks, including guest book talks, book trailers, audiobooks, and student book talks.

Table 1.3. Types of Book Talks

Book Talk Style	Teacher Directed?	Uses Outside Sources?	Includes Students?
Teacher book talks	*Yes.* You can even improv book talks without reading the book, using the back cover material or reviews on Goodreads, but this is not advised until you are a pro (or overtired and desperate).	*Sometimes.* You can use digital texts and read aloud the first page or two if you can't find a hard copy. You can use online reviews and cover art to engage your students.	*No.* You're speaking to students but not directly including them in the creation of your talk.
Guest speakers	*Not really.* You should give your guest speakers the general outline of a book talk included in this chapter, but after that, you're not directing this one.	*Yes.* This is where you invite anyone from the school or community into your classroom to talk about a book they like!	*Sometimes.* A quick survey of whom students want to invite to your classroom is a great way to ask people to come into your class since you can say a student requested them! You can also bring in former students as speakers, too.
Book trailers	*Not really.* After selecting the trailer, you simply push play. You may want to add some additional context before or after students view the trailer.	*Yes.* The internet has great resources; your librarians probably have great resources; and this book includes ideas in the appendix. Twitter rocks for this, too.	*Sometimes.* Check to see whether trailers exist for books your students like or ask/assign your students to create one. Tell them to be on the lookout for cool ones to bring to class.
Audiobooks	*Not really.* This is similar to book trailers. You find the clip, give some context, and let students enjoy!	*Yes.* If you don't already listen to audiobooks, you should! Ask your librarians, friends, or other teachers about them. And, obviously, the internet is full of resources, too.	*Sometimes.* Same as book trailers. Get kids as involved as you can!
Student book talks	*Not really.* If it's an assignment, you're outlining the guidelines and assessment criteria, but otherwise, it's all in their hands.	*Sometimes.* Students might turn to the internet or other people for ideas. Give them helpful guidelines in using outside resources.	*Yes.* This is one of the greatest benefits of this style. They take ownership of a story they like and share it with the class. They can do this as a full class presentation, in small groups, on discussion days, or all of the above.

When they're ready, students are great sources of book talks, too. A book talk is more authentic than a book report. It's not about proving that the student read the book or can summarize plot. Rather, students need to think rhetorically: What's the best way to "sell" the book to their peers? They need to think about book talks that have hooked them and apply the same strategies. How can they highlight the most significant moments without major spoilers? What excerpt can they read that allows the audience to get interested, but also leaves them needing to read more to find out what happens? Figure 1.1 is an example handout with guidelines for a student book talk assignment.

Heinemann/Fleck

Book Talk Guidelines

Outline: You will give a 2-3 minute book talk on a book you have read or are reading this semester. Your talk will tell us what the book is about and what you liked about the book. You will be assessed on both the content/information of your presentation and your presentation/speaking skills

Requirements:
Your book talk will be assessed on the following requirements on the REVERSE side.

Presentation
1. Bring the book itself and/or create a slide with images relevant to the book.
2. Use appropriate language (clear, articulate, loud enough, slow enough).
3. Use appropriate body language (stand up straight, make eye contact, use gestures if appropriate).
4. Organize information clearly and logically.

Reading - WHAT
1. Begin with engaging, effective introduction (attention-grabber) - You might choose to START with the excerpt!
2. Name author and title.
3. Read an excerpt to get us interested! For example, you could read your favorite passage, one that connects to your life, one that explains something really important about the plot or a character, one from the beginning that introduces the plot, and/or one that leaves us with a cliffhanger!
4. Explain the setting, main characters, and basic conflict without giving away any spoilers!

Reading - WHY
1. Tell us why you like it: How does it connect to your life? What interests you?
2. Choose the best audience for this book. Consider age, interests, reading level, etc.
3. Explain a theme. What are you learning from this book? What is the author saying about life?

Book Talks will begin on _____. This means you have ____ weeks to prepare! Names will be randomly drawn each day, unless someone volunteers. If you are absent when your name is called, you will be put back into the drawing. Think about the best book talks you've seen and channel that energy!

Figure 1.1. Book Talk Guidelines. *Courtesy of the authors*

For reluctant readers and voracious readers alike, book talks provide a lens with which to read and offer them an opportunity to share a story they love with others.

Engagement on Social Media

Whether or not you are active on social media, many of the authors that your students read are. Social media platforms, including Twitter, Instagram, and Goodreads, can be useful to engage students in literacy by helping them find new books, connect with writers, and communicate with a larger community of readers. On Twitter, for example, in 140 characters or less, you can tweet about your book talks and tweet directly to authors.

When students like a book, it's easy for them to tweet directly at authors to tell them how much they loved it. When students who claim to hate all books finally find one that makes them open to reading again, the author deserves to know. Many authors, especially YA authors, love hearing these stories and will respond to you and your students by liking the tweet you posted about them or directly messaging you about your students. Sometimes they might even offer extra books and sign them for individual students in your classrooms.

TEACHER TIP: AUTHORS WHO TWEET BACK

Andrew Smith @marburyjack
Rainbow Rowell @rainbowrowell
Robin Benway @RobinBenway
Meg Wolitzer @MegWolitzer
Jenny Han @jennyhan
Barry Lyga @barrylyga
Arin Andrews @arin_andrews
Huntley Fitzpatrick @HuntleyFitz

Take screenshots of the tweets and email them directly to students. Get ready for your students to reply with excitement (*"No way!* That's so cool!") because many high school students aren't used to this kind of interaction with adults, especially published writers. When students love a piece of art and the creator loves that they love it, this interaction changes how students think about books and their authors, too.

Figure 1.2. Tweets

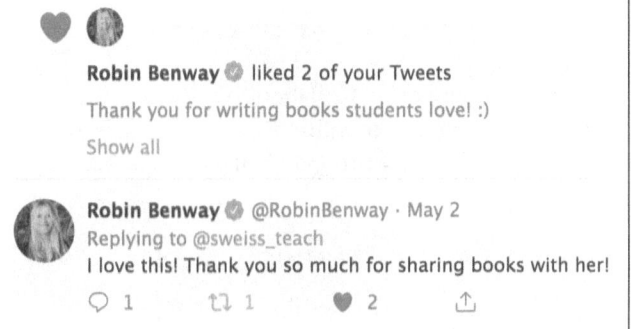

Figure 1.3. Tweets

STUDENT STORY: SELENA FANGIRLS FOR ROBIN BENWAY

Some of the most enthusiastic responses received about Collaborative Reader Workshop were from students that YA authors communicated with directly. Selena came into Mrs. Fleck's classroom determined to hate reading. No book had ever worked for her. No English teacher had ever made her read. She skimmed it all.

Then she found the book *Emmy & Oliver* by Robin Benway, and her whole universe shifted. She was so excited to read this book, frequently claiming she couldn't put it down and asking for extended reading time.

You know how students sometimes hide their cellphones in their laps to text? Selena hid *Emmy & Oliver* in her lap to keep reading.

When her teacher tweeted about this, Robin Benway not only did a special shout-out to her on social media—Selena actually jumped up and down about it in class when she found out—but she also sent her a personalized book.

Selena is now in college and regularly makes alumni visits. She still cites finding this book as one of the most "amazing" moments of her life. She not only loved a book but also felt loved in return, all because of a social media connection.

CLOSING THOUGHTS

The statistics about the decline of reading are alarming. But students will read if you let them—if you help them find the right book, set up a comfortable space to read, step away from the front of the room for a while, and give them time.

There are so many ways to fill your classroom environment with books and reading suggestions. When you connect on a human level with the readers in your classrooms, they are more likely to stop clinging to the idea that they hate reading. And when they see their teacher trying new genres and gushing about stories they love, they get a glimpse into how reading can stay with them into their adult lives.

Reading is the first component of Collaborative Reader Workshop. The next chapter explains how, once a month, students use their self-selected, independent reading as content for writing and analysis practice.

START PLANNING!

1. What resources does your school already have for getting books into kids' hands?
2. Where can you store books in your classroom?
3. Who are the readers on your staff who might want to share book suggestions with your students?

Chapter Two

The Writing

> One of the most important takeaways I gained from reader workshop was with writing. We were able to write about our books for a small audience and share with a new facilitator each time. It helped guide my writing toward literary works I was interested in. It held us accountable for our work by not only our teacher reading it, but being able to share it in small groups, and in ways that helped me prepare for future college writing assignments.—Meghan, former reader workshop participant

A room of students reading beneath dimmed classroom lights with orchestral music playing quietly in the background doesn't always look like teaching, especially to someone who isn't in your classroom every day. Sometimes a student-centered pedagogy seems "fluffy" to teachers who still prefer to teach in a traditional, teacher-centered model. Some teachers think students should listen to instruction during class time and save pleasure reading for home.

But the only way to make students into better readers is to let them read. The second part of this book explains why. For now, though, when someone asks, "But what do your students *do* with all this reading?" this chapter will help. Each month, your students will demonstrate their reading and writing proficiency in one-page analyses about their self-selected, independent reading books.

THE ONE-PAGE ASSIGNMENT

Once self-selected, independent reading has transformed your students into avid (or, at least, mildly interested) readers, you can introduce the writing assignments and discussions that bring purpose and focus to all the reading they're doing.

Here are the basic components of Collaborative Reader Workshop: self-selected, independent *reading* + one-page *writing* + collaborative *discussion*. Once a month, you can invite faculty and staff from around the school to join your students for small-group discussions about the books they're reading, books they want to read, and books they love. (The purpose and structure of workshop discussion days are detailed in chapter 3.)

To prepare for workshop discussion days, students write one-page responses inspired by Kelly Gallagher's model in *Readicide* (2009). As Gallagher and other advocates of self-selected, independent reading note, the best way to remove the joy from independent reading is to weigh it down with lots of annotations and written work. If you dedicate time to read, share tons of book talks with your students, and model the enthusiasm and critical thinking of an expert reader, your students will develop their own reasons and goals for reading without the need for frequent annotations or book reports.

But no system is perfect. So although an effective English teacher will try not to disrupt their students' reading, some students—especially struggling or reluctant readers—benefit from extra accountability. As Gallagher warns in *Readicide* (2009), "it's a delicate balance" (82).

There are also administrators, parents, and often students themselves who aren't convinced that reading is enough; they want to see more concrete growth. They want to know what students turn in. In short, they want to know, "What's the grade?" And though it might be preferable to do away with grades altogether, the real world demands working within the systems of that world.

So each month, during the week leading up to workshop discussions, students write a one-page response. Monthly one pagers don't disrupt daily independent reading but still give reluctant readers a reason to keep reading and, most importantly, provide a way for you to regularly assess their progress in reading and writing standards.

The term "one pager" is kind of a rhetorical trick: writing a page feels doable, no pressure. Even though students are practicing critical reading and writing skills on a monthly basis, these one-page analysis assignments don't cause a ton of stress because they aren't called "essays."

The short length is one way to keep one pagers feeling light. Another way is to continue to offer choice. Students have a choice about what they read for independent reading, and each month, they also have a choice from among twenty different prompts to demonstrate their reading and writing proficiency.

Kelly Gallagher in *Readicide* (2009) and Kylene Beers and Robert E. Probst in *Notice and Note* (2012) offer useful reading prompts. To provide opportunities for multiple learning styles, include creative prompts that ask readers to think about their books in new ways. For example, you could ask students to curate a playlist for a character in their book or create a piece of art to represent a crucial moment in the plot. Table 2.1 contains examples of one-pager prompt choices.

Not all students prefer reading literary or young adult fiction. Some pick up histories or biographies of athletes or musical artists. For example, Malcolm Gladwell's books *Outliers* (2008) and *David and Goliath* (2013)

Table 2.1. Sample One-Pager Prompts

	Fiction	Nonfiction
Sample prompt adapted from *Readicide* (2009)	If this book had one more chapter, what would have happened? This chapter could take place before, during, or after the action of book. Explain what would happen and justify it with evidence from the book.	If the author was going to write an updated edition of this book, what might she add to the argument? What has taken place in the world recently that would serve as effective evidence for the argument? Explain how it would impact the author's original argument.
Sample prompt adapted from *Notice and Note* (2012)	When the author interrupts the action to tell you about a memory, stop and ask yourself, "Why might this memory be important?" The answer tells you about the theme and conflict or foreshadows what might happen later in the story. Explain the significance of the memory.	Discuss a significant memory, piece of research, anecdote, or so forth that the author chooses to highlight. Stop and ask yourself "Why might this moment be important for the author's main idea or argument?"
Sample prompt by Fleck/Heinemann	Imagine that you have been hired to create a soundtrack for the film version of the book. Select eight to ten songs that you would include on the soundtrack and explain why you would select each song. Songs may connect with particular scenes, characters, settings, or themes.	Same idea: imagine that you have been hired to create the soundtrack for a documentary detailing the findings of the books. Select eight to ten songs that you would include on the soundtrack and explain why you would select each song. Songs may connect with particular chapters, discoveries, questions, or arguments.

Note: Kelly Gallagher's monthly prompts can also be found on his website: www.kellygallagher.org/instructional-materials.

---

16. One Pager: Soundtrack

Skills Assessed (*W indicates writing, *R indicates reading. Both tend to intertwine a bit)

- CCSS W11-12.1 Write arguments to support claims in an analysis of substantive topics or texts, using valid reasoning and relevant and sufficient evidence. *(aka answer the prompt questions, support it with evidence from your book, and explanation of those significant parts of the text)*
- CCSS.ELA-LITERACY.W.11-12.4 Produce clear and coherent writing in which the development, organization, and style are appropriate to task, purpose, and audience. *(aka your ideas come across clearly, are organized and logical, and show some development based on prompt)*
- CCSS.ELA-LITERACY.W.11-12.9 Draw evidence from literary or informational texts to support analysis, reflection… *(aka use ideas and examples from your book to support your thoughts and ideas about it!)*
- CCSS.ELA-LITERACY.RL.11-12.10 By the end of grade 11, read and comprehend literature, including stories, dramas, and poems, in the grades 11-CCR text complexity band proficiently, with scaffolding as needed at the high end of the range.

Title of Book: _____ Author: _____

Date Started/Completed: _____ Pages Read: _____

One Pager Prompt(s): Write (or type and print) a one page response to the following questions regarding your RBC reading thus far. Bring this response to our Fourth Friday discussion.

Imagine that you have been hired to create a soundtrack for the film version of the book. Select 8-10 songs that you would include on the soundtrack and explain why you would select each song. Songs may connect with particular scenes, characters, settings, or themes.

Nonfiction: Same idea! Imagine that you have been hired to create the soundtrack for a documentary detailing the findings of the books. Select 8-10 songs that you would include on the soundtrack and explain why you would select each song. Songs may connect with particular chapters, discoveries, questions, or arguments.

Write or type your response on a separate document and bring to class Friday. That means if you typed it, you have to print it!

REFLECTION: At the bottom of your response, describe the skills you focused on in this One Pager. Then reflect on how that has impacted you as a reader and writer.

ACADEMIC HONESTY: By signing below, I am indicating that I read/am reading the book, and the information on this page is accurate.

Signature _____

_{One-pager prompts based on *Readicide: How Schools Are Killing Reading and What You Can Do About It* by Kelly Gallagher (2009)}

Figure 2.1. One Pager: Soundtrack. *Courtesy of the authors*

are big hits for students who don't consider themselves to be "humanities" people. With this in mind, each one-pager prompt provides iterations for fiction and nonfiction books.

Assigning the One Pager

Let's talk about timing. Whereas some educators require their students to finish a book per month or a book per semester, the goal of Collaborative

Reader Workshop is simply to get students to read every day. You don't want to dissuade students from picking up that long Stephen King book or from challenging themselves with a novel by Dickens. And you don't want your students to stick with books that aren't working anymore. If they dedicate two weeks to a novel and then decide they're just not that into it, they can break up with the book without worrying that they need to rush to finish another one before workshop discussion day.

This means that students are often in the middle of a book when it's time to start preparing for workshop discussion day. That's okay! Almost every one-pager prompt can be addressed at any point in the book. For example, one prompt (listed in table 2.1) asks students to imagine another chapter of the book, but that chapter doesn't have to be tacked on at the end. Maybe they want the protagonist to have another run-in with a love interest before the big showdown near the end. Awesome! What would that look like? Where would it take place? How did the characters feel? The additional chapter can be added anywhere in the book.

Since many students use Collaborative Reader Workshop as a time to try out lengthier books, they may write about the same book for two (or even three) workshop discussions. That's okay, too. Since students will be writing on a different prompt each month, they won't lose any practice by closely analyzing multiple parts of the same book. In some cases, this leads to especially nuanced analysis.

Of course, every rule has an exception. If a student recently started a book and has read only a chapter or two, it might be difficult for them to answer some of the prompts about characterization and plot. Although you should encourage them to practice close reading by identifying what they can discover from the first few pages, they probably have more to say about the book they finished before picking up the new read. In this case, students can write on either book for workshop discussions.

Students also know that the monthly one-pager prompts never change. The only qualification is that they can't write on the same prompt twice. There are plenty of options, so there's no need to repeat. If they come across a moment in their book that they just *have* to write about, they can complete their one-pager response at any time—as long as it's ready for workshop discussion day. Collaborative Reader Workshop one pagers are "officially" assigned a week before the discussion day.

Here are questions that often come up: Is it enough for students to write about their self-selected, independent reading only once per month? Doesn't that mean they will read books that they will never write about? Yes. And that's okay. Adult readers do not write or discuss every single book they read. One of the flaws with traditional English instruction is that some teachers insist on assessing students' understanding of everything they read. However, if students are going to improve as readers, they need to read much more than what teachers can assess. Think of one pagers as a way to check in.

On the other side of the spectrum, some educators worry that assigning a one pager every month is *too* much. These teachers make a gesture toward providing student choice and differentiation by setting aside one unit, usually at the beginning or end of the school year, for students to pick their own books and complete a book report project. Isn't that enough?

Ask your students about this kind of work. What you'll hear from more than one student—often with a sense of pride—is that they read a book, or part of a book, back in eighth grade and then reused the same book report every year. As if not reading—and getting away with it—is a good thing.

As their current teacher, you want them to know this reading space is different, not because you want to trick them into actually reading a book, but because you want to provide them with authentic reading experiences. Rather than assessing whether a student can summarize the plot of a book for a book report, you want to know what they think about the characters in the same way you ask them about their friends or family. You want them to analyze why the author would choose certain words or pieces of language in the same way that they might consider levels of meaning in the words of a break-up text message.

In a Collaborative Reader Workshop model, one pagers provide a consistent purpose for yearlong independent reading and allow for consistent practice in reading analysis.

Connecting to Whole-Class Content

Although it's always legitimate to ask students to write about what they're reading, one-pager responses are also a way to supplement and reinforce the content you're studying as a class. For instance, in a composition course, include prompts that reflect the elements of craft being studied. You could ask students to craft text conversations between characters of their choice, read to work on dialogue, analyze descriptions of setting, or identify an argument and explain how the author provides evidence and analysis to support his or her claims.

The same goes for literature study. You can frame one-pager prompts around literary concepts being discussed in the context of the whole-class novel. If your American literature class is reading *The Great Gatsby* and discussing how Fitzgerald develops his critique of the American dream through specific details earlier in the novel (e.g., ashes that take the form of men in the valley of ashes, the butler's nose, etc.), you might invite students to look for similar details that develop themes in the self-selected reading.

This way, students are not only practicing literary analysis in a large group but also applying what they're learning to books of their choice. By pushing themselves to consider how a device works in multiple texts, they strengthen their proficiency in literary analysis and in writing.

ONE-PAGER ASSESSMENT

One concern of teachers new to Collaborative Reader Workshop is that there's no way to read all the books students are reading and writing about. How do you know they're actually reading? How do you know they're writing accurately about what they read?

This is one of the perks of shifting to a student-centered model of literacy instruction: In traditional literature study, teachers spend a lot of time translating plot. In Collaborative Reader Workshop, the teacher's interpretation of the text isn't central to the instruction; it can't be. Sure, it might be easier for English teachers to tell their students what and how to think, but students learn best when they have a chance to think about a text on their own terms first.

So you trust your students to think deeply about whatever they're reading and, whether or not you have read the book, you can assess their writing (Is it focused? Organized? Grammatically correct?) and reading (Is their response supported with evidence? Developed? Thorough enough to be clear to someone who hasn't read the text?).

Since there is an inherent overlap between reading and writing skills, there are many ways to assess student writing. You probably have had students who write clear, grammatically correct claims that make no sense because they hadn't completed the reading. In the same class, you might have another student who has written a really thoughtful analysis that is buried in unorganized paragraphs, sentence fragments, and spelling mistakes.

Collaborative Reader Workshop keeps things simple, using the one-pager response as a way to assess students' mastery of basic skills in both writing and reading. Since a student's chosen prompt varies month to month, the rubric is simple and consistent. For writing, the rubric addresses the following three skills:

- *Idea/focus*—Is the response focused on one idea? Is it accurate?
- *Organization*—Is the response logically organized with multiple paragraphs that transition between ideas and develop these ideas throughout?
- *Language*—Is the response free of significant errors?

And for reading, the one-pager rubric assesses these three skills:

- *Evidence*—Is the claim supported by accurately cited textual evidence?
- *Reasoning/inference*—Is the response thoughtful? Does it show an understanding of how an idea has developed?
- *Summary*—Does the response include key concepts and details and omit unnecessary ones?

One-Pager Rubric				
Standard - WRITING	Exemplary	Mastery	Proficient	Developing/Emerging
IDEA/FOCUS Response is focused: Address the chosen prompt with clear, accurate ideas or claims. *Develop the topic thoroughly by selecting the most significant and relevant facts, concrete details, quotations, or other information and examples appropriate to the audience's knowledge of the topic.*	5	4	3	2 1 0
ORGANIZATION Your ideas come across clearly, are organized within paragraphs and throughout the text, and show development based on prompt. *Produce clear and coherent writing in which the development, organization, and style are appropriate to task, purpose, and audience.*	5	4	3	2 1 0
LANGUAGE Language has variety in sentence structure, demonstrates consistent use of precise word choice, and is free of significant errors that detract from the quality of writing. *Produce clear and coherent writing in which the development, organization, and style are appropriate to task, purpose, and audience.*	5	4	3	2 1 0
Standard - READING	Exemplary	Mastery	Proficient	Developing/Emerging
EVIDENCE Cite strong and thorough textual evidence to support analysis of what the text says explicitly as well as inferences drawn from the text. *Use ideas and examples from your book to support your thoughts. Explain how the evidence supports your claims.*	5	4	3	2 1 0
REASONING/INFERENCE Analyze how and why individuals, events, or ideas develop and interact over the course of a text. *Explain how (and why!) a character or idea has changed as you've been reading.*	5	4	3	2 1 0
SUMMARY Summarize key supporting ideas and details. *Tell your reader what they need to know about the plot and characters to understand this book, but don't over-explain!*	5	4	3	2 1 0

Total: _____/30

Note: Summative Assessments receive a 15 point Writing Score and a 15 point Reading Score.

Figure 2.2. One-Pager Rubric. *Courtesy of the authors*

The rubric isn't a secret. Students have access to it from the beginning of the year. The consistency helps struggling readers and writers know what to expect in their writing. It's always the same skills, which means both the teacher and student can easily identify areas in need of improvement. If students are struggling to get started or can't sustain their ideas for more than a couple sentences, check out table 2.2 for a few go-to strategies to get them started.

Table 2.2. Brainstorming Strategies

Strategy	Overview	Types of Students This Strategy Helps Best
Quick write	1. Give students a set amount of time (three to five minutes). 2. Have them time themselves or listen to a song about that length. 3. Tell them to write without stopping for the *entire* time, focusing on their chosen prompt. 4. Scaffolding: For severely struggling students, break the prompt down into smaller questions or ask students to start by writing about what they noticed and then go back to the prompt. It may help to write beside them. 5. After they have written for that set amount of time, repeat until they have words on the page that can be organized into the start of a response.	• Students who struggle with starting but will keep writing once they're on a roll • Perfectionists who want to get it right the first time. This allows them to write without getting caught up in editing and revising • Students who struggle with writer's block
Teacher conference	1. Have students meet with you individually when they have started a draft. 2. Walk through their response, giving suggestions to develop their ideas based on the prompt and the rubric. 3. Scaffolding: For students who struggle to write but can communicate their ideas clearly verbally, offer to type as they talk to get them started.	• Students who benefit from one-on-one direct instruction • Students who can get started but struggle to develop their ideas • Students who have ideas but freeze when they have to put anything on the page
Teacher model	1. Choose a prompt and handwrite or type while the students watch. 2. Do it "quick write" style at first to show students that not everything you write is solid gold, either.	• Students who benefit from or who need direct teacher instruction • Students who struggle with self-starting

(*continued*)

Table 2.2. Continued

Strategy	Overview	Types of Students This Strategy Helps Best
	3. Ask students for suggestions to develop your response based on the prompt/rubric. 4. Demonstrate revision and formatting in your finished product.	
Peer-led writing groups	1. Put students in their Collaborative Reader Workshop discussion groups. 2. Make sure they have the rubric in front of them. 3. Direct strong student writers in each group to guide peers through quick writes, additional development points, and sharing ideas.	• Students who are collaborative by nature • Students who are interested in leadership • Students who respond better to peers than adults

Although it's important for students to understand what is expected of them for one-pager assignments, it's even more important that they understand that these key writing and reading skills will be expected of them outside of school, too. No matter what professional or educational step they take next, they will need to be able to communicate their ideas in an organized and appropriate way. The one pagers help them practice this communication with a book they enjoy.

What the Students Think

Metacognition is key. In order to retain what they learn, students need to be self-aware of their own thinking and learning. So at the bottom of each one pager, students are prompted to reflect on the literacy skills—both reading and writing—practiced during the previous month's independent reading and writing: "At the bottom of your response, describe the skills you focused on in this one pager. Then reflect on how that has impacted you as a reader and writer."

This allows students to not only concentrate on teacher feedback but to home in on the skills they focused on and then apply them beyond the assignment. It encourages students to think past the grade and pushes them to contemplate who they are as readers and writers and where they can grow. Allowing them space to reflect on how they are growing throughout the process creates an authentic application of skills and understanding of how reading is strengthening both their quality of life and their academic skills.

HOW ONE PAGERS SUPPORT DISCUSSION

One-pager responses push students to think more deeply about their self-selected reading, reinforce literacy skills being practiced in other units, and hold reluctant readers accountable. These are all reasons for teachers to love one pagers. Your students, however, will like them for another reason: writing a one pager means coming to workshop discussion with something to say.

Many people—yes, even adults—get a little nervous when they are called upon to speak in group settings. Knowing this, ask your students to complete *and print* their one pagers before class and bring them to discussion. In one-to-one schools, you may allow students to use their computers to reference their work, but because screens can be incredibly distracting during a conversation, it's a better idea to ask your students to print or handwrite their work in order to have it during discussions before turning it in at the end of the class period.

Your students may struggle at first to complete and print their one pagers before class starts, but it's a point worth insisting on. When students have their ideas, supported with evidence, right in front of them during discussion, every person in the group has something to contribute. Tell them this. By communicating this purpose to students, you help them to understand that you are not assigning busywork. You are modeling and giving them practice for how to show up prepared. This is how they should attend classes, business meetings, and any other group situations as adults: ready with a meaningful contribution.

Will some students ask you to print out their one pager at the last minute? Of course. Will some students try to write theirs during that day's ten minutes of independent reading? Obviously.

As with all procedural expectations, you will deal with these individual students on a case-by-case basis. Maybe one of your students has a part-time job after school and then needs to put their little brothers to bed before waking up and getting them ready for school. For that student, it might be necessary to complete the one pager right before class. In that case, you might print it out for her or allow her to complete it by the end of the day.

But when another student admits to being "too lazy" to finish or had to do math homework instead, it doesn't make sense for them to use reading time to complete the work now. After all, it's the time and space to enjoy a book that matters most in Collaborative Reader Workshop. So letting the one pager take the place of reading defeats the purpose. Plus, that student needs the natural consequences of not having anything to say during a discussion where others are prepared.

As always, communicate with your students. Let them know that you are not upset with them and do not want to punish them. Rather, you want to help them practice being prepared for group work. Remind them that it's important for them to write the one pager because it's a way for them to explore an idea connected to their book and contribute effectively to a collaborative discussion, and it's also a way for you to check in on their writing and reading skills.

CLOSING THOUGHTS

Writing and reading go hand in hand. Allowing students the space for both is part of the beauty of Collaborative Reader Workshop. Writing about what they are reading independently not only offers choice (students choose the text and the prompts) but also gives them concrete practice with the demands of effective writing, stretching beyond the classroom and into their lives postgraduation.

This is why writing is an important component of Collaborative Reader Workshop. It's one way for students to think deeply about their reading and form habits in doing so for their futures. The next chapter explains another way: by discussing their self-selected books and one-pager analysis work in small-group, collaborative discussions.

START PLANNING!

1. What skills do you want your students to have additional practice with?
2. Do your students have access to computers to type their one-page responses? If not, how will you assign and collect this work?
3. How do you want your students to reflect on their growth?

Chapter Three

The Discussion

> As a social studies teacher, I can see students' reading interests and promote a broad range of genres and modes through reader workshop discussions. Most importantly I build a better, broader, stronger rapport with students. When I participate in workshops, our large school becomes a nurturing community. After engaging in reader workshops I'm not just "some teacher" to those students. I am a reader who also happens to teach.—Cary Waxler, high school social studies teacher

Let's start with how discussion days *feel*. Once a month, students drop everything else they're working on—and stressing over—to sit in a circle and talk about books. Even though students are practicing critical literacy skills during these discussions, they still think of this day as a "break" from English class. Because it is different from the normal routine, class suddenly seems a lot less like class and more like a chill conversation with friends.

Although many literacy educators advocate for one-on-one conferences between teachers and individual students to support independent reading, Collaborative Reader Workshop takes this collaboration a step further: once a month, students participate in book club–style discussions about their self-selected reading with small groups of other readers. This chapter explains the purpose behind giving students time to discuss their self-selected reading in small groups and the procedures to help it go smoothly.

DISCUSSION DAY STRUCTURE

Discussion days foster a sense of community in the classroom that extends far beyond those days and far outside of your classroom. In the traditional, teacher-centered model of education, the most frequent instructional method is lecturing (Goodlad 2004, 105). Most teachers say they want their students to feel like members of a community, but most classrooms aren't structured to help create that feeling. Instead, the teacher usually talks to the class as a whole group, and students usually work independently. In fact, when you walk into a typical high school classroom, there's a fifty-fifty chance that the students will be engaged in passive learning: listening as opposed to reading or discussing (Goodlad 2004, 123).

The discussion days of Collaborative Reader Workshop actively reject this model of education and work toward fostering community among students and among students and adult readers. On discussion days, the English teacher invites outside faculty, staff, and community members into the classroom to facilitate—not lead—the discussions.

The basic structure of discussion day is always the same.

Table 3.1. Discussion Day Agenda

Book talk (5 minutes)	Whole class	The classroom teacher, a student, or one of the guest facilitators shares what they're reading with the whole group. This is a great opportunity for students to hear talks from other teachers and staff.
Independent reading (10 to 15 minutes)	Individual	Since independent reading is the focus of discussion days, this might be a day to give your students extra time for independent reading. This gives additional time for facilitators to join the class as well.
Quick write (5 minutes)	Individual	Each discussion day has a focus. The quick write is a way to get your students to start thinking about the focus. It also creates a starting place for the collaborative discussion.
Collaborative discussion (20 to 25 minutes)	Small group	With an adult facilitator, students share and discuss ideas from their quick writes, one-pager responses, and books.
Reflection (5 minutes)	Individual	Try to save a few minutes at the end of the period for students to reflect metacognitively on their discussions: what did they get out of it today? This reflection can take place on Google Forms, a sticky note, or the back of their printed one pagers.

1. Book talk
2. Independent reading
3. Quick write
4. Collaborative discussion
5. Reflection

Before starting your book talk, remind students that other book lovers will be joining the class for the day's discussions. Although you may invite your facilitators to join the class at the start for independent reading—teachers need a break from the hustle of the school day, too!—make sure they know to make their way to your classroom within the first fifteen or twenty minutes of class. And if someone's running late, no problem—that means your students get extra time to read.

Discussion Focus

To bring direction to the collaborative discussions, each discussion day has a literary or craft focus, usually one that aligns with whatever is being studied as a whole class. This focus serves two purposes: first, along with the one pagers, the discussion focus creates another opportunity to supplement whole-class lessons or units.

If, for example, students are reading *The Narrative of the Life of Frederick Douglass* and students have been analyzing how Douglass uses the symbol of a ship to emphasize his oppression, the Collaborative Reader Workshop discussion might ask students to think about how the authors of their independent reading books use imagery or other literary devices to develop the themes. It's an opportunity for additional practice: students can write and think about the whole-class unit of study through the lens of a text that they chose and enjoy.

Second, since every student is reading a different text, the discussion focus provides a structure for readers to form connections among disparate books. If one student is reading *To All the Boys I Loved Before*, another is reading *Winger*, and a third is reading *Pet Sematary*, they can all talk about how the author sets the scene in the exposition in their separate novels, how characterization is developed, or how conflict works out during the resolution. When a student thinks about how a concept like characterization works in multiple texts, they are practicing valuable critical thinking skills: recognizing differences and similarities, identifying patterns, and making abstract connections.

Although it's important to back your students' right to direct their learning by allowing them to choose among a variety of writing prompts, you can

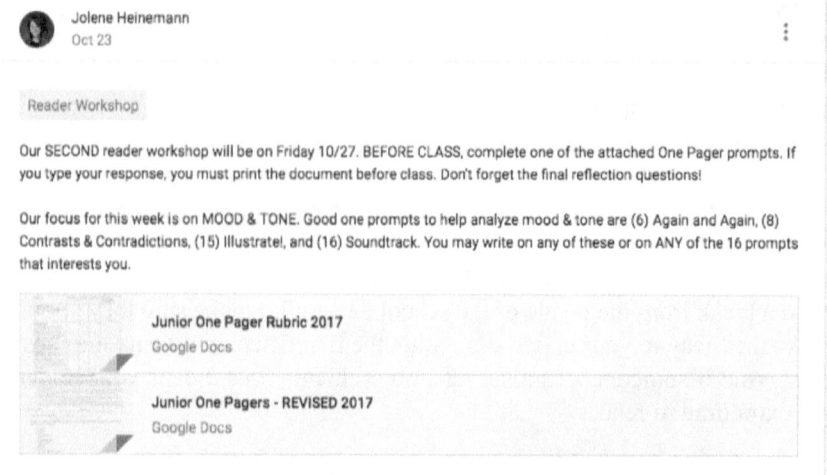

Figure 3.1.   Reader Workshop. *Courtesy of Jolene Heinemann*

recommend specific one-pager prompts for those who want to prepare for the discussion focus. If the class has been studying mood in whole-class texts and the workshop discussion focus is on mood, let students know ahead of time which one-pager prompt will help them practice mood. Figure 3.1 shows a Google Classroom post that reminds students that discussion day is coming up and suggests one-pager prompts.

Although upholding the student's right to choose what they write about is one of the core tenets of Collaborative Reader Workshop, there may be times when you assign specific prompts based on the discussion focus. In the weeks leading up to the SAT, for instance, you may insist that your students' one-pager work aligns with rhetorical analysis, the type of writing they will be doing for the SAT essay. It's okay to be flexible when planning your discussion focuses.

Quick Writes

If you prefer to give your students full choice when it comes to their one-pager responses, the quick write is another way to get them thinking about the discussion focus. A quick write is a short burst of timed writing in which students (and teachers—always model writing!) write in response to a prompt without thinking too hard about it. The quick write is a strategy to get thoughts on paper without editing, revising, deleting, or worrying. For reader workshop, it allows students and facilitators to tap into the day's discussion focus.

Additionally, whereas the one pagers are formal pieces of analysis, organized effectively and supported by textual evidence, the quick writes are creative and

Table 3.2. Discussion Focus and Quick-Write Prompts

Discussion Focus	Quick-Write Prompt
Characterization	Imagine a character (or speaker, if you're reading nonfiction) from your book showing up at our high school. What groups would they be part of? Who would they be friends with? What classes would they take? How would they dress, speak, act, etc.?
Conflict	Consider a central conflict of your book. Write a conversation between two characters/people in the story in which they talk about the conflict(s) in your book. The characters do not have to come to a resolution, but they can—it's up to you. Possible formats: dialogue out loud, text message convo, social media exchange, phone call
Language and style	As you read today, locate one line that stands out from your book. This line may stand out because it has literary devices (symbol, simile, metaphor, hyperbole, etc.), creative dialect, especially emotional, funny, or distinctive tone, beautiful ideas, or so forth. Write your line on your sticky note. Stick your sticky note on the back of your one pager and imitate it in a sentence of your own. Try to imitate the literary devices, structure, word choice, dialect, tone, and so forth—whatever you found appealing about it.
Theme	Imagine that your book's protagonist (or author if you're reading nonfiction) is giving a talk at our high school based on this book. What is the talk about? Why?
Setting	Draw or describe a scene or map from the book you're reading. Include any details that bring this place to life in your mind. These details can come directly from the book or from your imagination based on what you've read so far.

fun, offering students another way to think about their text. Table 3.2 lists a variety of discussion focuses, along with their corresponding quick writes.

Quick writes also give facilitators—both students and adults—an additional talking point for the collaborative discussion. So, even if a student did not complete the one-pager response, that student still has at least one idea to contribute to the discussion. The quick write serves as an access point to jump-start the collaborative discussions.

Collaborative Discussions

After students listen to a book talk, enjoy reading quietly for a while, and use a quick write to start thinking about that day's discussion focus, shift them into the activity that brings it all together: the collaborative discussion. Discussions are a time for students to think deeply about what they're reading, but discussions also offer essential practice with speaking and listening skills.

Students must listen to other speakers in order to make connections and build on their ideas. Most importantly, discussions allow students to connect with other readers, both classmates and adult facilitators.

The National Council of Teachers of English (2018a) agrees that English curriculum shouldn't merely start and end with the book: "In effective schools, instructional conversations about how, why, and what we read are important parts of the literacy curriculum." Although the classroom teacher models this thinking through book talks and one-on-one conferences throughout the year, these interactions are not enough. Collaborative Reader Workshop discussions create a regular opportunity for students to discuss how, why, and what they read with each other and with adults whom they don't usually see as readers.

Although Collaborative Reader Workshop discussions are meant to be flexible and free flowing, it's useful to provide a general structure to get things going, especially with facilitators who may not be English teachers. One possible structure looks like this:

1. Share and discuss quick writes. This helps students think about the discussion focus.
2. Share from one pagers. All students should come to discussion with their ideas prepared in their printed one pagers.
3. Chat about books in general.

Let's be honest, though: chatting about books doesn't always come naturally at first. So provide a list of ideas for your students and facilitators to refer to. Figure 3.2 shows directions that could be projected at the front of the room during discussions. If your students start losing steam, they always have ideas for something to talk about next.

Discussion Agenda

1. **Talk about today's discussion focus: language & style**
   a. Share your quick write about a line you liked and how you imitated it!
   b. Describe the language of your book OVERALL: What is the tone? Does the author use literary devices? Does the author use humor, satire, dialect? Is it formal or informal? What else?
   c. Evaluate the language. How does the language impact the message?
2. **Share parts of your one pager analyses!**
3. **Share about our books in general!**
   a. What's going on currently?
   b. What do you like/dislike/have questions about?
   c. Do you need a new book for winter break?
   d. ANYTHING ELSE

Figure 3.2. Discussion Agenda. *Courtesy of Jolene Heinemann*

The Discussion 37

Similarly, it's important to provide your facilitator with an outline of how the discussion might look, including additional talking points like the following:

- If you were to cast characters in a movie version of your book, who would you pick and why? (If there is already a movie, do you agree with the casting?)
- Who is the most relatable character?
- Are there characters you dislike? Explain.
- If your character(s) is in high school, describe how you believe they will be as an adult. If your character(s) is an adult, describe who they were in high school.

A sample facilitator guide can be found in figure 3.3.

Collaborative Reader Workshop - Facilitator Info
Meeting 3 Focus: Language/Style

Thank you for taking time out of your day to come discuss books with my junior students! Take today's discussion in whatever direction you would like, but if you get stuck along the way, here are some suggestions....

- **Share your Quick Write!**
   - As you read today, locate one line that stands out from your book. This line may stand out because it has:
      - Literary devices (*symbol, simile, metaphor, hyperbole, etc*), *Interesting structure (stream-of-conscious), Creative dialect, especially emotional, funny, or distinctive tone, beautiful ideas, etc*
   - Write your line on your sticky note! Stick your sticky note on the back of your one pager and imitate it in a sentence of your own! Try to imitate the literary devices, structure, word choice, dialect, tone, etc... whatever you found appealing about it.
   - When you finish, write a sentence or two explaining what stands out to you in this line and/or how the language helps the writer accomplish his/her purpose (to entertain, inform, persuade, etc).
   - FACILITATORS, Feel free to share a line from your book as well!

- **Today's Discussion Focus**
   - Share your quick write about a line you liked and how you imitated it!
   - Describe the language of your book OVERALL: What is the tone? Does the author use literary devices? Does the author use humor, satire, dialect? Is it formal or informal?
   - If you're reading a nonfiction text, how does the author use ethos/pathos/logos?
   - Connect to what we're learning about rhetoric! How does the author's use of language or style (including word choice, rhetorical devices, tone, etc) help them to fulfill their purpose (even if that purpose is just to entertain us)?

- **One Pagers**
   - Start with this week's focus! Did anyone write on the "Style File" prompt?
   - Share specifics of the one pager students completed for today! (They each wrote on a self-selected topic connected to their text.)

- **If conversation about today's focus dries up, here are more Possible Discussion Questions:**
   - What have you read about in your book so far?
   - How do you like the story? Characters? Setting?
   - What's the most interesting thing you've read so far?
   - If you were to cast characters in a movie version of your book, who would you pick and why? (If it's a movie, do you agree with the casting?)
   - Who is the most relatable character?
   - Are there characters you dislike? Explain!
   - If your character(s) is in high school, describe how you believe they will be as an adult. If your character(s) is an adult, describe who they were in high school.
   - ANYTHING ELSE YOU CAN THINK OF

Notes For Fleck/Heinemann:

Figure 3.3.   Collaborative Reader Workshop—Facilitator Info. *Courtesy of the authors*

If the discussion doesn't follow this structure, that's okay, too. Some of the most effective discussions go "off script" when readers start talking about movie adaptations, music, life goals, and more. What matters here is that you are allowing your students to engage in reading in multiple ways and make authentic and meaningful connections with others.

In *Reading in the Wild* (2014), Donalyn Miller outlined the benefits of reading communities in the classroom (98), explaining that they:

- Foster connections among readers
- Increase how much readers read
- Challenge readers to try new genres and writing styles
- Increase readers' appreciation of what they read
- Encourage mindfulness about what readers read

Although Miller allows these communities to form naturally in her middle school classroom, Collaborative Reader Workshop is a way to explicitly construct these communities among students and among students and adults.

After participating in workshop discussions, students begin to see reading as a desirable pastime, something that their friends, social studies teacher, and coaches do, too. Although daily book talks are effective ways to introduce students to new reading material, some students, especially hesitant readers, take recommendations from friends and mentors much more seriously than the recommendations that come from their English teacher. And there's nothing better than hearing that a friend loved the book you recommended: their appreciation makes you feel more connected to the book. Discussion days offer time and space for students to make these connections.

PREPARATION FOR DISCUSSION DAYS

To prepare your students for discussion, there are several key elements to consider.

1. Facilitators—how you will invite guests into your room to facilitate the discussions
2. Group dynamics—how you will build the groups based on the students in your class
3. Reflection—how you will build time for your students to reflect on the discussion

Facilitator Engagement: How to Recruit Facilitators

Bringing staff, faculty, and community members into your classroom on a regular basis is one of the best things you can do to build a unique and interesting classroom environment. You should introduce discussion facilitators not as discussion leaders but as guests, as other book lovers who are here to talk about books. Facilitators may ask questions to keep the conversation going, prompt students to elaborate on a claim, lead team-building activities, and share stories (and laughter!) with the group.

Try to bring in a variety of facilitators: teachers from other departments, administrators, community members, former students, and so forth. One of the goals is to show your students that English teachers aren't the only adults who read. Take the time to survey your students about who they want to invite. When staff members know they were requested by a student, they are often more convinced to participate.

HOW TO FIND FACILITATORS

- *School librarians*—This is the first place to look. Library educators already love books and your school. Ask them for help with book talks, facilitator discussions, and so forth. Make sure your students know and appreciate all they do to encourage reading.
- *Teacher friends*—Contact any ready and willing colleagues that you know students enjoy or that you know are avid readers. Sometimes convincing colleagues who are *not* avid readers can be a great experience, too! (Don't underestimate the persuasive power of baked goods.) Aim to bring in facilitators from a variety of departments and content areas so that students see that not only English teachers are readers.
- *Student services and counseling staff*—Contact your school's counselors, social workers, deans, or other student support staff. Educators in these roles are often excited to join the classroom environment to further their relationships with students since they don't see them every day. You can create even more productive discussion groups by placing students who struggle with time management, self-control, or social emotional issues with those qualified to help, especially when these students never may have sought out these relationships on their own. Joe Molly, dean of students at Barrington High School, makes a point of joining every reader workshop he can—even when he needs to come in late or leave early to deal with disciplinary issues. "The connection I make with kids is much different when I talk about reading," Joe explained. "We make a connection that goes way beyond my role as a dean. It's a conversation."
- *Administrators*—Ask the principal, superintendents, associate principals, the school police officer, and department chairs (from all departments). Administrators often want to know what's going on in teachers' rooms, and welcoming them in on discussion day helps them understand the value you bring to your students and the school. Since they don't have as

(continued)

> ## HOW TO FIND FACILITATORS (*continued*)
>
> many opportunities to interact face-to-face with students, most administrators appreciate the chance to build relationships within the student body. Everyone wins.
> - *Community members*—If there is an old movie theater in town that all the kids go to, invite the owners. If there are popular baristas at a coffee shop they all frequent, request they come—with coffee. If your students' parents have time to come, bring them in! This is another way to show your students that reading is a lifelong habit.
> - *Former students/alumni*—Nothing quite compares to discussions led by beloved former students or alumni. These students know the drill since they participated as readers when they were in your class, and a student facilitator allows groups to feel as if they are functioning even more independently since their facilitator is close to their age. This also provides leadership experience to former students and allows current students to see that these skills go beyond the class. Again, everyone wins.

Once you've figured out who to recruit as a facilitator, how do you get them to show up? The first step is to shoot off an email to entire groups or to individual staff members based on student requests. To make it easier on your facilitators, you may just ask them to reply to the email with periods available if they're interested and then create a schedule. This takes a lot of frontloading on your end but may remove a barrier that prevents facilitators, especially new ones, from taking the extra time to sign up.

> Hello, all:
>
> Each month, I put together reader workshop discussions for my junior college prep classes, and this is my annual invite asking you to join us.
> My students are always reading a self-selected book on their own. To add purpose and rigor to their self-selected reading, once a month, they write a one-page close reading analysis about their book and participate in small group discussions. Since they are all reading different books, each month's discussion has a skills focus (characterization, conflict, etc.) to give focus to the discussion and allow students to make connections among texts.
> All you have to do is bring a book you're reading and have a conversation about reading with a small group of kids. We start the class with ten minutes of reading and a quick write, so you can join any time in the first fifteen minutes and then duck out five minutes before class ends to beat the bell. I will send you a list of discussion prompts the day/morning before to help guide discus-

sions, but if they go off topic, that's not the end of the world. My primary goal with reader workshop is to create positive experiences surrounding books.

This semester's discussions will be on "first Fridays": **[insert dates here]** during **[insert class periods here]**. Please let me know if you are available to join us for any of these classes. If you're not sure about a date right now, I am very willing to keep bugging you before future workshop discussions. :)

Even if you don't teach English classes, we hope you can join us! Students love to see teachers from other departments talking about books.

Let me know if you'd like to join. I appreciate you and your time!

Thank you!

P.S. If you know any other faculty or staff interested in Collaborative Reader Workshop who weren't on this email please forward this email or let me know!

Alternatively, if you already have a go-to group of facilitators who have agreed to help or have participated in years past, make it easy on yourself and include a sign-up document in your email. Either way, teachers are busy people, so make sure to send out a reminder the day before that includes the discussion agenda, identifies that day's focus, and reminds them when and where to meet.

If facilitators are (understandably) hesitant to give up precious open time to join your workshop discussions, try a few of these talking points:

- *It's only twenty minutes.* Although they may join earlier to read with your class, they don't need to be in the room until the discussions start and can slip out afterward.
- *If a student requested them, remind them.* Teachers don't want to disappoint their students.
- *Their participation helps them connect with students outside of their own classes.* It's always easier to build relationships that aren't dependent on grades.
- *Recreational reading correlates to higher achievement in all class periods.* By contributing to a culture of literacy, facilitators are working toward academic excellence across all content areas.
- *You will bring them baked goods.* Don't underestimate the power of bribery.

Group Dynamics

Once you have facilitators, it's time to think about how to create your student groups. The way you do this depends on your specific school context and the needs of your students. Chapter 1 provides options for ways to organize independent reading to meet different needs.

Similarly, the way you structure group dynamics is dependent on your particular group of students and may differ from year to year or even from unit to unit. When grouping students, consider the best opportunities for collaboration in your classroom. This doesn't always mean putting students with others whom they are familiar with.

Table 3.3. Student Groupings

Group Style	Pros	Cons
Grouping by level or interest	• You have similar reading levels in one group, so can pair them with a specialized facilitator (i.e., a librarian with reluctant readers, a reading specialist with struggling readers, an English language learner [ELL] teacher with ELL students, etc.) • Grouping by interest means students will often be reading similar kinds of books, which makes it easy to share suggestions. • Students may be more comfortable with each other because of common interests or skill levels.	• Grouping by level risks creating a "classroom within a classroom" vibe in which high level readers know who they are, lower level readers know who they are, and so forth. • Students are less likely to be exposed to other kinds of genres or topics. • Grouping by topic can limit the range of books being read and recommended.
Mixed groups (not separated by levels or interests)	• Any group can be placed with any facilitator. • Each group discusses a diverse range of books. • Higher level students can model thinking and discussion skills for lower level students. • Students may challenge each other to explore books they would not have thought of otherwise.	• Struggling readers can get by without sharing much. • Higher level readers may not feel challenged enough. • Some facilitators may not meet specific needs of students. • Students may break into subgroups based on similar interests, leaving some students out of the discussion.
Student-chosen groups	• Students feel that they have ownership over their learning. • Students are more comfortable with each other. • Students may end up choosing to read the same	• Facilitators may need to deal with more management issues. • Discussion is more likely to go off topic. • Students may be more tempted to plagiarize work rather than share ideas.

Table 3.3. *Continued*

Group Style	Pros	Cons
	or similar books, which creates natural connections among books. • Students may be more interested in reading books recommended by their friends.	
Mixed groups with student requests	• Students feel that they have ownership over their learning. • The teacher can make final decisions on groups (i.e., if student A wants to be with student B but only because they're friends and have no common interests or reading preferences).	• Students may focus too much on whom they want to be grouped with and lose sight of reading focus. • Teacher may feel additional stress to create groups that match all student requests.

If you think about the strongest literary communities you've ever been a part of—by choice or through assignment in school—the group probably challenged your interpretation of texts based on experiences outside of your own and introduced book suggestions you never would have known about or sought out yourself. Discussion days also give students opportunities to talk and connect with students they may not otherwise interact with.

Reflection

When you look around the room at groups of students talking excitedly with adults, it can be tough to put a halt to these discussions. In some cases, you may decide that it's best to allow your students to continue their discussions until the bell that day. Other times, you may want to make sure your students have time to reflect that day.

Whether you make the time after discussion or at the beginning of class the next day, make sure to set aside class time for students to internalize all that they discussed. You can accomplish this by prompting them (via written instructions, Google Forms, verbal instructions, etc.) to think about:

- Which books do they want to add to their reading list (hard copy or Goodreads)?
- How did they participate in discussion? Were they simply listing off plot points about their book or did they really get into describing it to the group? Did they ask questions or bring up new ideas?

- How can they add to their one-pager reflections to recap what they talked about during the day's discussion?
- Should they update the book they are currently reading on Goodreads or add friends from their discussion group?
- What connections did they find among the multiple texts shared during discussion?

Though there are many different ways for your students to reflect on their discussion, the basic purpose is to challenge them not to simply share but also to *think* about how they are contributing and how they can improve their participation in their reader community.

CLOSING THOUGHTS

Collaborative discussion is the part of Collaborative Reader Workshop that students most look forward to. It allows them to deepen their understanding of what they read not only by explaining the books' plot points to others but also by exploring how the books made them *feel* and why people should read them. If they dislike their books, their fellow readers could give them suggestions for new reads, right then and there.

Workshop discussions are also an opportunity for students to talk to people in class that they may otherwise not interact with and to see their teachers or deans or coaches as readers—and people!—instead of authority figures. It builds a sense of community through the shared interest of stories not only within the classroom but within the larger school context.

When a student starts saying "hi" to their discussion facilitator in the hallway and talking to their science teacher about a book they heard about in discussion, they begin to think of other people as readers. Ultimately, with support, they will come to an understanding of their own identities as readers. They become better readers and writers because of these discussions, but maybe more importantly, they become more engaged with the stories and people around them.

START PLANNING!

1. How will you need to help your students prepare for discussion?
2. Who can you invite to facilitate these groups?
3. How can you most effectively group your students?

Chapter Four

How to Confront Challenges

> As a busy classroom teacher, sometimes the prospect of giving up prep time for anything seems daunting or obligatory, but participating in reader workshop has been invigorating because it is an authentic experience. Reader workshop often feels like a book group among friends—and my group is made up of sixteen-year-old boys!—Laura Minerva, high school English teacher

When other English teachers hear about reader workshop, their responses follow a similar pattern: "That sounds cool, but . . . "

But.

That "but" is everything for teachers. Teachers are always juggling dozens of balls at once: lesson planning and grading and answering parent emails and figuring out how to handle that classroom management issue and sponsoring extracurriculars while also meeting administrative expectations and, on top of everything else, trying to have a life outside of school.

So when someone tosses another ball at you, as much as you may want to catch it, sometimes it seems impossible to take on one more thing. You tell yourself everything you're already doing is good enough. The kids are getting something out of it. They're learning. It's working. Why risk compromising the whole juggling act by trying something new?

All teachers know that it's exponentially easier to teach a course the second, third, or tenth time around. Since this is your first time setting up Collaborative Reader Workshop in your classroom, this chapter is here to help by identifying common concerns and suggesting ways to address those problems.

CHALLENGE 1: I CAN'T GIVE UP THE TIME!

You don't have to be a veteran teacher to realize that "English language arts" is a *huge* subject. We are responsible for helping our students master an enormous variety of skills in one course: narrative writing, informational and literary analysis writing, argumentative and persuasive writing, research writing, rhetorical analysis writing, the revision process, effective style and grammar—and that's only writing.

Add in multiple types of reading and speaking skills, the historical and cultural context of the literary works, social-emotional learning (SEL) practices, and time to pre-assess, formatively assess, and summatively assess all of these skills and concepts, and it's not surprising that the planning can feel overwhelming. And for every lesson you plan, how many are you brushing over or sidestepping, assuming (or hoping) they will be covered in later courses?

It's true that setting aside time for students to read in class means less time for other activities or lessons, ones that are valuable and worth your students' time. The thing about Collaborative Reader Workshop, though, is that it doesn't simply help students pass a test or even a course. It can change lives by showing "nonreaders" that they just haven't found the right book yet. It can develop habits of mind that continue far beyond the classroom.

An often-cited statistic reports that the average high school student reads only seven minutes per day (NEA 2007). When they do read, 58 percent of students try to multitask with other forms of media (i.e., by watching TV shows or browsing online) some or most of the time (NEA 2007, 43). Since reading requires sustained attention and intentional questioning, multitasking is detrimental to successful reading, yet this is how most our students read!

Think about it this way: if students don't have time to read in your class, they may never learn effective reading habits. The National Endowment of the Arts calls this a matter of "national importance" and not without reason. As chapter 8 examines in detail, research shows that reading is the best way to improve comprehension, vocabulary, reading speed, spelling, grammar, and writing style. In fact, it's the most effective way for students to increase overall academic achievement (NEA 2007, 13).

CHALLENGE 2: MY ADMINISTRATION REQUIRES I TEACH SPECIFIC WHOLE-CLASS BOOKS

Literacy educators differ in their beliefs about the effectiveness of whole-class texts compared to the differentiation inherent in a workshop model. For example, whereas Nancie Atwell encourages a full workshop model consisting of self-selected, independent reading for all extended texts and short excerpts as whole-class models, Gallagher and Kittle (2018) value the "synergy—a level of insight—that occurs when an entire class huddles around a core text" (63). Reading whole-class texts creates a space for students to grapple with complex language and to discuss their ideas in groups, a practice that generates diverse thought.

In schools with strong vertical and horizontal alignment, teachers don't always have the freedom to make their own curricular choices. If the goal of education is to help students apply what they've learned in one class to another class (and ultimately throughout the rest of their lives), it's important to develop a scope and sequence so that teachers understand what students learned the year before. But that sometimes means that the curriculum simply isn't flexible.

Fortunately, although Collaborative Reader Workshop can stand on its own as a model for students to study and discuss books without requiring every student to read the same book, it's also flexible enough to work alongside and in between whole-class texts—a point that needs emphasis since most high school English departments mandate specific titles.

In districts that ask students to read novels as a class, teachers can use Collaborative Reader Workshop to supplement whole-class units of study. For example, some teachers use Collaborative Reader Workshop between whole-class units to ensure that their students are always reading a book. The daily reading stays the same, but during whole-class units, students spend this time reading the class text. If students finish the assigned whole-class reading ahead of time, they have a novel to return to during daily independent reading time. This means that students get more practice reading, thinking critically, and writing clearly without time spent on direct whole-class instruction.

Alternatively, some teachers ask their students to read two books at a time: one for pleasure and one for study. After all, as Gallagher and Kittle (2018) note, most adults read more than one book at a time, a practice also expected in college (48). When the class is reading a novel together, self-selected reading becomes the students' weekly homework. It's also possible to set aside one day of the week—a Monday or Friday, for example—for self-selected, independent reading while the remainder of the week focuses on whole-class study.

Remember, too, that Collaborative Reader Workshop discussions give students an opportunity to make connections among multiple texts and, often, multiple genres. Let's say a student is independently reading *All American Boys* by Jason Reynolds and Brendan Kiely while studying *To*

Kill a Mockingbird as a whole-class text. By thinking about the role that race plays in twenty-first-century police brutality issues, students can make contemporary connections to Tom Robinson's trial in *To Kill a Mockingbird*. They didn't lose understanding of the whole-class text by having independent reading time; rather, they gained the ability to make comparisons using information from multiple literary texts, a skill emphasized in the College and Career Readiness Standards.

Since Collaborative Reader Workshop has a different focus each month, you can deliberately align one month's focus with skills being practiced in your current whole-class unit. If you're talking about direct and indirect characterization in *Of Mice and Men*, ask your students to think about direct and indirect characterization in their self-selected book, too. If students are learning about the rhetorical situation, ask them to consider how the authors of their self-selected books build their message. If students are writing personal narratives, ask them to consider how the authors of their self-selected books begin and end their stories, make their characters realistic, or establish setting.

Nothing in the whole-class curriculum has to change. Collaborative Reader Workshop shouldn't take time away from the curriculum; rather, it should build on it by giving your students an opportunity to apply what they're learning to another text.

Collaborative Reader Workshop is flexible. If you want to devote more time to self-selected books, you might have students meet biweekly; if you are hesitant to give up a lot of class time to dive into a monthly structure, your students may meet in discussion groups every other month. And if you aren't sure how to balance self-selected, independent reading books with a whole-class novel, a three-week mini unit is an effective compromise, allowing student readers to focus on one novel at a time but still benefit from having choice.

How your students juggle multiple books is up to you and your class, but it's important to note that adopting Collaborative Reader Workshop into your curriculum doesn't mean giving up whole-class books. Depending on how you structure your class's workshop, you may not be able to discuss as many elements of a whole-class novel as you did in years prior.

Although that may feel like a loss, consider what you're gaining. You're reminding students that books are a joy. You're compromising with those students who can't get into *Jane Eyre* by setting aside some time for them to read a book they *can* get into. You're creating a space for students to improve their reading stamina and interest level, which helps them when it comes to full-class text study.

So really, you're not giving up anything.

STUDENT STORY: OLD SPORT FINDS HIS READING SPACE

One year, the junior classes' monthly Collaborative Reader Workshop discussion fell at the end of a week during which students were finishing a characterization project for *The Great Gatsby*. Trying to be considerate of our students' time, their teachers didn't assign a one pager about independent reading for the sake of the discussion. Instead, they allowed the students to use their one-pager assignment as an opportunity to expand on their analysis of characterization in *Gatsby* and then talk through this work with their small group and adult facilitators during the discussion.

Since the classes had already developed a strong community of readers, students understood that using the time to talk about *Gatsby* in tandem with their independent reading books was helpful in understanding the characters. This discussion also gave them the opportunity to "teach" their facilitator about everything they were learning—and as we all know, explaining a concept to someone else often clarifies our own thoughts and ideas.

CHALLENGE 3: I DON'T HAVE THE BOOKS

You can't run an effective Collaborative Reader Workshop without high-interest books for your students to read. The National Council of Teachers of English (2017) has written extensively about the importance of classroom libraries, which allow students to practice selecting and evaluating their independent reading materials, skills that foster engagement in the reading community.

How you acquire the books for your classroom library takes a bit of work, but it isn't impossible. Teachers have found success buying bargain-priced books at Salvation Army, Goodwill, and other resale shops. Frequently, local libraries—and even your school library—give away books as they make way for new purchases. Many of your students' families are willing to donate books if you send out an email with the course syllabus at the start of the year or request donations during back to school night.

Chapter 1 explores additional ways to build your classroom library. It might make sense to take a year to prepare before fully incorporating Collaborative Reader Workshop in your room. In the meantime, you may have to depend on your school library to get books into your students' hands.

CHALLENGE 4: IF I COULD ONLY GET THEM TO READ!

It's normal to question whether kids will even read during independent reading. "Fake reading"—a phenomenon all English teachers are familiar with—is so easy. The kid zoning out, staring off into space. The kid scrolling through his cell phone in his lap or behind the book he's holding upright. The kid who picks a different book off the classroom shelves and flips open to a random page every day. By giving these students time to fake read, aren't you wasting their time?

Before you panic and throw independent reading out the window, stop and consider how many students are actually fake reading. Teachers, especially highly reflective ones, are quick to think a lot about the two or three students who are off-task rather than the twenty or more who are focused on the task at hand, immersed in their books. So try to reconfigure the question. Don't ask yourself, "Am I really willing to allow those three kids to sit and do nothing for ten minutes?" Instead, try this: "Am I willing to take reading *away* from twenty kids, preventing them from building a habit that may impact them for the rest of their lives?" Isn't that an easier question to answer?

We also need to be realistic about our students' attention levels during a traditional lesson. Think about your own high school experience. Did you pay attention every moment, writing down every idea the teacher shared and practicing skills with full efficiency during each period? Of course not. When teachers present material though lecture, even if they utilize student-centered tools like PearDeck and GoGuardian, they rarely have the full attention of every student in the room. When a class is discussing a whole-class novel, the teacher rarely has participation from every student. You may try your best to create engaging, relevant lessons, but sometimes, a student is just having a bad day.

This is true for independent reading, too. Students' reading rates may change day by day, depending on their mood. Maybe they didn't have time to eat breakfast this morning. Maybe they have a test next period that's stressing them out. Maybe they just got into a fight with a friend. We need to remember that our students are humans, not machines. Ideally, everything runs smoothly every day, but we don't live in an ideal world.

It's also important to be cognizant of a text's Lexile score. The same student reads at slower or faster rates depending on the complexity of their chosen texts. You can help your students understand their reading rates and set reading goals based on those rates. One simple way is to hand students a sticky note on their way in the room. Ask them to write down their name, the book they're reading, and the page they're starting on. After ten minutes of reading, direct them to figure out how many pages they read in ten minutes and multiply that number by five to figure out how many pages they should be able to read in a school week. Explain that there's no shame in a slower rate because it's not a competition. Students read at different rates, and those rates change depending on the books they choose.

By teaching your students to regularly calculate and report their reading rates, you can track how much they're reading on a weekly basis and, consequently, whether they're fake reading. Let's say a student should be able to read about fifty pages in a week. If that student is on page 41 one Monday and then only on page 56 the next week, you know it's time to check in with him about his book. Does he like it? Is it time to try something new? Is she getting distracted? These one-on-one conferences show your students that you notice them and you care about them and their progress.

If they enjoy their book but still find themselves getting distracted, help them problem solve. Often the culprit is their cell phone. So it's your job to help them make healthier decisions about their technology use. Rather than demand that they put away their phone ("Because I said so!"), ask them—earnestly—whether they want you to hold on to their phone for them so they can enjoy their book without distraction. You will be surprised by how many students are happy to hand you their device, especially when they trust that you will return their property to them at the end of the period.

Most students, though, will refuse your offer. When they do, ask them if they're sure. Tell them you think it will help but allow them to make the decision. It's okay if they choose to put their phone in their backpack instead. The point of this conversation is to show that you care. You won't remove their phone simply as a punishment, but you will offer them support as they develop the habits of a reader. And remind them, too, that after graduation it will be their job to manage their devices for college and career environments. Your classroom is a great place to start training their minds to do this.

But it doesn't take a phone to distract someone. Sometimes our minds just aren't in it. This may be more difficult for some teachers to swallow, but maybe zoning out and doing nothing is exactly what a student needs one day. In our technology-driven world, young people don't often have time to sit and do nothing without the continual entertainment and distraction of a screen. Research shows that boredom leads to self-reflection (Zomorodi 2017). When we let our minds wander, we practice problem solving and creative thinking. We construct narratives about our lives, identifying what has led us to where we are now and where we want to go next. It's when we have time to think—without distraction—that we construct our identities.

Chapter 10 talks more about how Collaborative Reader Workshop fosters social-emotional learning, but for now, don't be alarmed if a student is having trouble concentrating during reading time one day. Check in with them, sure. Encourage them to keep reading. But if they can't—or won't—then allow them to enjoy the time as meditation and be comforted that you have created a space that allows for quiet reflection.

And when students are bored with their book but won't admit it—or maybe don't even realize it—hand them another book. As a fellow reader who gets excited about books, you aren't there to judge them for abandoning a book or forgetting it at home. You're there to put another book in their hands and to assure them that all they have to do is try it. If they don't like this one, there are dozens more to try next.

Ultimately, you are not there to make sure a student reads an entire book or makes it through a list of classics. It's tempting to obsess over how much they're reading or how many books they finish but allowing them choice is not about making it a competition. It's about helping them build lifelong reading habits.

In the end, if a student reads only bits and pieces of a bunch of books without ever building a consistent habit, know that your work hasn't been in vain even for that student. You modeled a reading life. You brought in other adults who love to read to show that reading isn't a hobby exclusively for English teachers. You introduced dozens, if not hundreds, of books. You created a welcoming space for students to take risks with new books. And maybe, years from now, when such students finally find books that speak to them, they will remember the space you created, how comfortable it was, and how much you cared that they become readers.

When that matters to you, it's amazing how much more it can matter to them, in your class and beyond it.

CHALLENGE 5: WHAT IF THEY READ SOMETHING INAPPROPRIATE?

Should students be allowed to read whatever they want? What happens when a high school junior chooses *Diary of a Wimpy Kid*? Or reads about smoking marijuana in *A Visit from the Goon Squad*? Or masturbation in *Diary of a Part-Time Indian*? Or a sex scene in any number of romance novels? What do you say when that angry parent calls, aghast at the book found in her child's backpack?

Here's what the National Council of Teachers of English (Right to Read, 2018c) says: "To deny the freedom of choice in fear that it may be unwisely used is to destroy the freedom itself."

One of the primary goals of Collaborative Reader Workshop is to create lifelong readers. Lifelong readers know what they like: they're practiced in selecting novels that will hold their interest and know when it's better to abandon a book to move on to the next one. And sometimes that means a teenager is going to want to read about sex or drug use or violence. Although you may choose not to store these books in your classroom library, it's important that you respect students' right to be selective when it comes to their personal reading, even—and especially—if it doesn't align with your own tastes.

Controversial books also offer a safe means for students to explore the real world outside of the classroom walls. If you allow students to read only books deemed "safe" by traditionalist communities, you place yourself in a "morally and intellectually untenable position" of being dishonest and inauthentic about "the nature and condition of humanity" (NCTE, Right to Read 2018c). Not only do we want to promote joy in reading, we also want to give our students a chance to think deeply about the topics that matter to them and that will continue to matter to them after high school graduation.

To approach controversial texts proactively, you may want to send home a letter or email that outlines your stance on censorship and invite parents to reach out to you about their specific concerns. Ultimately, a student's reading habits will be influenced by their home lives. You can provide research and recommendations from organizations like the National Council of Teachers of English, but what is deemed appropriate for one family may differ from what is deemed appropriate in another family. You may provide guidance, but the decision is ultimately between the student and their families.

STUDENT STORY: SHANNON READS SCANDALOUS STORIES

Shannon couldn't control herself. She was turning red and hiding behind her book, trying—and failing—not to burst out laughing. Laughter is contagious, and other students were starting to pick up the vibe.

The source of her outburst quickly became clear when she passed her book to the girl sitting next to her, pointing with enthusiasm at a specific passage. Ms. Heinemann walked over to investigate.

"What's up?"

She stifled her giggles. "Nothing."

"Hmmm." Ms. Heinemann pressed her. "Whatcha reading?"

Not without a bit of embarrassment, Shannon held up her book: *Fifty Shades of Grey* by E. L. James.

Here's the thing, though: Shannon wasn't a reader. Ms. Heinemann had handed her two different books over the past week, and after reading the first few pages, she had rejected them. Too boring. Yet here she was, almost a hundred pages into a novel. Sure, it was a novel of questionable content and of even more questionable literary merit, but she was reading. Her older sister lent it to her when she was home from college the weekend before, and they'd been texting about it all week.

Ms. Heinemann made a mental note to help Shannon find love stories with better prose but then smiled and shook her head.

Ask yourself: If her teacher had taken that book from Shannon, would that have made her a better reader?

CHALLENGE 6: I CAN'T FIND FACILITATORS

Sending out that first email invite is tough. Your colleagues already work so hard: grading during their lunch periods, planning at night after their own children are in bed, and making time to incorporate new administrative initiatives each year. How can you ask them to give up some of the little time they have left to help out in your class?

For any project to be successful, the creator needs to consider how it may meet the diverse needs of multiple community members. As an English teacher, your primary purpose for inviting colleagues and community members into your room is to improve your students' reading and writing proficiencies by encouraging a love of reading and providing an authentic audience for their thoughts. But for the administrators, coaches, and teachers from other departments who are invited into your room, literacy is only one of many issues they're dealing with throughout their day and probably only one of many reasons they agreed to participate in Collaborative Reader Workshop.

Counselors and social workers, for example, may use Collaborative Reader Workshop discussions as an opportunity to make a connection with a struggling student or to introduce themselves to students they might otherwise never see. A teacher from another department may want to build a more positive relationship with a student who is creating a management issue in his or her classroom. Administrators may simply value the opportunity to get out of their office and into a classroom.

This is why you don't need to feel guilty about asking your colleagues to give up a free period: you are not the only one who benefits from bringing guests into your room for Collaborative Reader Workshop. Facilitators consistently report that their favorite part about participating is the relationship building. As teachers, how often do we get the chance to make connections with students that aren't overshadowed by a grade? When facilitators see a student from Collaborative Reader Workshop in the halls, they have something to say to that kid. They smile and greet each other and ask how the reading is going.

Community is important, and as you know by now, one of the goals of Collaborative Reader Workshop is to create a community of literacy within the school community. And for science teachers or deans to give up forty minutes of their day to talk to your students about books, they need to see the individual as a whole person, not simply as a kid who needs to learn science or a kid who needs to behave in class. This is why it's okay if a Collaborative Reader Workshop discussion drifts away from books. If you're going to build community, students—and facilitators—need to find joy in these discussions, and sometimes what they enjoy is talking about that new TV series everyone is watching. Chapter 11 delves deeper into how Collaborative Reader Workshop builds community.

Although the community-building element of Collaborative Reader Workshop is inherently valuable, it isn't always possible to express all of this in an email invitation. But there are ways to make sure you have enough facilitators. Start with one partner: colleagues who are interested in starting Collaborative Reader Workshops in their classrooms or librarians. That way, even if there's a day when no one else can join, at least you'll have one additional adult reader in the room to talk about books and rotate among the small group discussions.

Librarians and English teachers are obvious starting points, but think outside the box about who you can bring in. If your school has academic coaches, make use of them! Invite former students to come back and lead a discussion; this is a leadership opportunity for them and a way for you to utilize the credibility that comes from an older student. Invite parents and community members. Chapter 3 discusses additional ways to encourage participation from colleagues around the school.

A final way to adapt Collaborative Reader Workshop is to depend on your students. Each month, a group could nominate a student leader to facilitate the discussion. In this format, rather than facilitating a discussion yourself, you would rotate and listen in. You can also supply students with sentence starters to help move the discussion along. These can be phrases such as:

- I think my book is interesting because . . .
- I'm not really feeling my book because . . .
- I noticed . . .
- When [student name] talked about _____, it reminded me of . . .

CHALLENGE 7: THE KIDS HAVE NOTHING TO SAY TO EACH OTHER

Have you ever been part of a book club that seems to exist as a reason to drink wine and socialize? When one member tries to direct the conversation toward the book, no one has anything to say. Struggling to find something to say about the book is an authentic experience, and you picked up this book about Collaborative Reader Workshop because you want to provide your students with real-world literacy experiences.

It's okay if students struggle to get started in discussion, but you can also make proactive decisions to help them connect with each other. Community doesn't just happen. It's possible that after you take the time to form student groups based on interest, match those groups with appropriate facilitators, and prepare an engaging quick write to match the day's discussion focus, the kids still have little to say.

Here's where team-builder activities come in. At the start of the semester or after forming new student groups, use team-builder activities to get students comfortable with each other and with their facilitator. Although it's easy to worry that you're wasting academic time, making recommendations for each other and asking questions of each other is often a necessary step if you plan to have these groups work together throughout the year. You need to make sure all students feel comfortable expressing themselves.

You could choose to keep it simple: ask your facilitators to begin each discussion with a nonacademic icebreaker. The group could whip around the table and talk about their pets or their favorite musical artists. Typically, once a student speaks the first time, it is easier for that student to speak up again. Alternatively, you could begin the first discussion by asking groups to come up with a group name or a logo. These simple activities help students to feel that they are members of a community, a team.

If you have more time, though, or are meeting more frequently, it's worth the time to start with a team-builder game to allow students to practice speaking up in discussion and to give them a chance to know each other. Table 4.1 lists some fast and easy team-builder activities to help your readers get started. Rather than leading or simply observing these activities, the adult facilitators should join in, allowing students to get to know them as well.

Table 4.1. Team-Builder Activities

Team Builder	Instructions
Minute in the hot seat	• One person is the timer and puts one minute on their phone. • Each group member (including adult facilitators) takes a turn in the "hot seat." • The teammates ask the person in the hot seat a bunch of quick-fire questions. • The person in the hot seat answers the first thing that comes to mind. • The person in the hot seat can always say "pass."
Scavenger hunt	• Hide some strange objects around the room or make a list of things already in the room. • Give the team three minutes to find as many items on the list as possible. • No one can leave the room to acquire items. • No one can take items from others without their permission.
Would you rather?	• Give the team a list or PowerPoint of "would you rather" questions and a set amount of time to answer them. • Can be used multiple times with different questions as a fun routine to start discussions.
Candy colors	• Hand out candy in different colors or flavors. • Assign a specific fact to each color and have groups share these facts with each other based on the colors that they have. • Facts could include: favorite color, family information, childhood memory, favorite food, movie most recently seen/watched, etc.

It's likely that the first couple Collaborative Reader Workshop discussions will follow the IRE structure: the facilitator initiates a *question*, a student *responds*, and then the facilitator *evaluates* or comments upon that response. One of the year-long goals is to break this format by pushing students to listen and respond to each other, instead of simply waiting for their turn to speak. Participating in a collaborative discussion is an academic skill and, like writing an essay or any other academic skill, can be developed and mastered with scaffolding and practice.

CHALLENGE 8: WHAT IF A STUDENT IS ABSENT ON DISCUSSION DAY?

Here's a reminder: not every classroom activity requires a grade. The best assessment—formative assessment that provides suggestions for growth—happens before a serious grade is entered into the grade book.

Yes, Collaborative Reader Workshop involves grades. The one-pager analyses detailed in chapter 2 are assigned a grade based on a rubric that measures students' proficiency in three reading and three writing skills. This is an opportunity to provide both rigor and purpose to students' self-selected, independent reading while also creating an opportunity for you to give feedback for students to apply immediately to their next one-pager responses.

The discussion, however, is worthwhile even without a grade attached, since it allows for community building and fosters positive experiences surrounding literacy. You do not need to assign a speaking and listening score to this discussion; in fact, students may feel more willing to express themselves comfortably in a discussion if they're not concerned about losing points.

If students are absent on discussion days, tell them you missed them. Then ask them to tell you about their book, collect their one-pager response, and encourage them to make sure they attend the next discussion day. If it becomes a pattern, investigate further to discover what struggles they may face in group settings. Your job is not to make sure that every activity is in the grade book but to provide them the support they need to grow.

CHALLENGE 9: IS THIS REALLY TEACHING THEM ANYTHING?

When you're new to independent reading and Collaborative Reader Workshop, you may wonder if it's even working: Is it too fluffy? How do I know whether they're getting anything out of it?

It's hard to give up control of your classroom, but it's also important to recognize that students need time and space to practice adult literacy skills.

Traditional English teachers spend more time talking through the plot than helping students practice literacy skills. Without giving them time to read and talk about books in class, you can't know that they will ever have that opportunity. Daily independent reading and monthly Collaborative Reader Workshop discussions create a space for students to practice thinking critically about a text without explicit teacher guidance. And if you don't give them this time, who will?

Even though it might be easier for teachers to teach only whole-class novels that they have "all figured out," students won't learn to think critically if they are being told what to think, and they won't become better readers if they read only books that are too hard for them. Rather than always answering their teacher's questions about a novel and repeating what they heard the teacher say in class discussion, students need to learn to come up with their own questions, ones that provide purpose for their reading other than the fact that the teacher told them to.

If you buy in to independent reading but worry that a reader workshop approach depends too heavily on a reader response attitude that accepts all responses regardless of critical thought, start by insisting that students back up their claims with textual evidence in their one-pager analysis responses *and* during workshop discussions. Although you want to encourage students to feel comfortable voicing their own values and sharing their own experiences, remind them to ground their ideas in the text.

The second half of this book explains why you should stick with Collaborative Reader Workshop. Collaborative Reader Workshop will improve your students' academic achievement (chapter 7), improve their social-emotional competency (chapter 8), work toward equity (chapter 9), and make your students lifelong readers (chapter 10).

CHALLENGE 10: I DON'T KNOW WHERE TO START

This is an easy one. Start by brainstorming a whole bunch of books that you love or think your students will love and figure out how you're going to get them into kids' hands. Plan a few books to "book-talk" to your students.

Then contact your school librarians and find out when you can take your classes to pick out books. When you're in the library, be proactive. Follow students down the aisles and ask what they like to read about. If they say they don't like to read, then ask what they do like to do. Use the librarians or online resources—Goodreads is a great one—to find a book for the kid who likes basketball or the one who wants to try a murder mystery or the one who reads only graphic novels.

TRICKS AND TIPS FOR FIRST TIMERS

Accept that it's going to be messy.

- Be flexible. A facilitator might back out last minute. That's okay! Now you have slightly larger groups. A student may forget to print their one pager. That's okay! They can still participate based off today's reading and quick-write prompt.
- Be part of a group. Although this chapter has focused primarily on relationship building among students and faculty from around the school, this is a space for you, too, to show students your interests and humanity.
- Say thank you. Facilitators are giving up valuable time in the name of literacy. End every discussion by asking your students to thank their facilitators, and make a habit of leaving written thank-you messages from you and your students. Candy and baked goods definitely sweeten the deal since the facilitators were "so sweet" to come in to your classes!

And keep this in mind: no one is stuck with a single book. When students pick up a book, they are simply trying it. If it doesn't work out, they can always try something else. Your goal is to get a high-interest book into each kid's hands. And then another. And then another.

CLOSING THOUGHTS

Setting up Collaborative Reader Workshop takes a lot of work. Outside of the discussion day, you have to send different email invites to different groups, keep track of a monthly schedule, send appointment reminders and discussion prompts, and write tons of thank-you notes.

It's easy to question whether it's worth the time, if you can't just let them read quietly and call it a day. But you have a responsibility to make all of your students into better readers while they're in your class. If you don't find a way to let them read and write and talk about books, you are not making them into better readers.

START PLANNING!

1. When is the best time for students to read in your class?
2. How many whole-class texts are you required to teach? And how can you help your students juggle two different kinds of reading?
3. What are you going to say to the parent or administrator who wonders if Collaborative Reader Workshop is worth the time?

Chapter Five

How to Make It Work for Your Students

> Collaborative Reader Workshop is a unique experience in the co-teaching setting because students who would usually only work with their peers in a special education setting are able to collaborate with peers in a general education setting, which is beneficial for all involved (including their teachers).—Dave Udchik, special education teacher

Teaching is hard. There's no one-size-fits-all solution. English department meetings are often loud places: English teachers would be happy arguing for hours about how to educate our students. Whether we should teach the book or the skill. Whether it's necessary to give reading quizzes to make sure students read. And whether vocabulary or grammar practice have any effect on writing.

The point is this: what works best for one teacher may not work for you. What works best for you one year may not work the next. Teachers need to be flexible and responsive to the students they have in front of them.

Depending on your objectives, you will vary the structure, focus, or procedures of Collaborative Reader Workshop to meet the needs of your students. This chapter offers suggestions for making it work.

DIFFERENT PURPOSES FOR DIFFERENT UNITS

Your instructional choices don't matter if you don't know where they're leading. Backward design, also known as "understanding by design," requires educators to first identify their specific objective: what is it you want your students to learn or understand? Once you know that, you can consider how you'll know that the student met that objective, and only then—after you know what they're learning and how they're going to demonstrate that learning—can you plan the steps that will lead students to this end.

Collaborative Reader Workshop is going to look different depending on your end goals, and those end goals likely will vary throughout the year as your students become more proficient with some skills or habits of mind and demonstrate a need for practice with others.

Focus on Love of Reading

For college preparatory and lower achieving students, the initial goal of Collaborative Reader Workshop is simply to encourage the enjoyment of reading. You don't want to overwhelm them with specific literary elements or close reading skills because that can take the joy out of reading.

Knowing that your objective is to get students to love books, your monthly discussion focuses and one-pager prompts could be broad at first: describe your reading life, identify and set goals about your reading habits, determine the genres you enjoy and the genres you'd like to try. As the year progresses, perhaps you move into the study of basic literary elements, like analysis of the development of characterization, conflict, and theme. These elements are the focus of the one pagers described in chapter 2.

To encourage a love of reading, especially in students who identify as nonreaders, you also will want to carefully consider how to engage them in group discussions. Can you pair reluctant readers with voracious readers who might recommend a book to win someone over? Can you invite their favorite teacher or coach? Or instead of teachers, maybe you want to invite senior students to serve as discussion facilitators, an arrangement that would benefit both the seniors as leadership experience and a resume builder while helping Collaborative Reader Workshop feel more rooted in the student community.

As students become more proficient at sharing in groups and backing up their thoughts with evidence from their self-selected texts during discussion, you also may shift the leadership opportunity onto the students themselves, allowing groups to appoint facilitators and determine a focus area for future discussions based on their interests at the time. Sometimes groups even choose to read the same novel to create a common experience that more closely resembles a book club in the world outside of education.

It may be beneficial to have students complete a reading questionnaire or even write a literacy narrative to share at their initial Collaborative Reader Workshop discussion in order to get to know themselves and each other as readers before shifting the focus into literacy practice.

Focus on Reading Skills

Although Collaborative Reader Workshop one pagers and discussions are an ideal way to push students to identify and analyze the significance of basic literary elements (i.e., exposition, characterization, plot, theme, resolution), you can easily adapt it into a more engaging way to study reading skills. In lower level classes in which struggling readers may be learning to decode and comprehend lower Lexile texts, your one-pager prompts could focus on identifying and understanding a feature of the text, rather than analyzing it. These comprehension prompts still can foster interesting conversation in Collaborative Reader Workshop discussions.

> *Prompt for more proficient readers*: How does the protagonist's characterization impact the themes and ideas of the novel as a whole?
> *Prompt for less proficient readers*: How is the character described? What do they look like? What is their personality like? Would you want to hang out with this person? Why or why not?

Educator Jacqueline Darvin (2009) discusses an after-school reader workshop program that teaches students to develop "literacy objectives" that foster metacognition. A student may, for example, want to practice visualizing ideas while they work toward self-monitoring their comprehension while reading (45). In their monthly reflections, students could also self-assess their progress toward their literacy goal and determine whether they need to change their goal for the next month.

Focus on Collaborative Discussions

Although the primary purpose of Collaborative Reader Workshop is building literacy and a love of reading, this structure also offers an opportunity for explicit practice with discussion techniques. The adult facilitator is an important participant in building community, yet his or her presence often leads to an initiate-response-evaluation (IRE) mode of communication that takes the shape of a spoke: The facilitator asks a question. A student responds. The facilitator comments on something that student said and poses a new question. Then the next student responds.

Again, if your objective is to give students a venue to gush about what they're reading and learn about new books, then defaulting to the IRE model doesn't hinder that purpose. Students are still in a different setup talking about books. Success! However, if one of your curricular goals is to push students to discuss more efficiently—to use evidence to support their claims, to listen and respond to other speakers' ideas, and to contribute without waiting for "their turn"—then you need to be more explicit about teaching these skills and directing students to practice them.

This is not to argue that these discussion skills must be formally assessed during Collaborative Reader Workshop discussions. Formal assessment of students' spoken contributions would create a logistical problem—how can you be everywhere at once and still facilitate your own discussion?—and, more importantly, would add an additional stressor to an activity that's supposed to joyous.

However, if effective collaborative discussion is important to you and you want to help students practice those skills even when not being observed by you, there are low-key strategies to push this participation. It's important, after all, that your students know that you don't teach collaborative discussion skills to make them squirm. You teach them because they will be in discussions for the rest of their lives (and usually without a teacher checking off that they make thoughtful responses to other speakers). They might as well use Collaborative Reader discussion days to practice these skills.

STRATEGIES TO ENCOURAGE COLLABORATIVE DISCUSSION

- Ask students to write down one (or more) question(s) to ask about other students' books. Challenge each student to ask at least one question of another reader per discussion.
- Assign one student as documentarian for each discussion. The documentarian tallies up how many times each participant talks or creates a map with lines from speaker to listener so that students can visualize whether the conversation is dominated by one person or more democratic. Figure 5.1 shows what this might look like.
- Give each student three stickers or sticky notes. At the end of the discussion, ask them to celebrate collaborative discussion by awarding their stickies to the students who made the best contributions. They must recognize at least two different students.

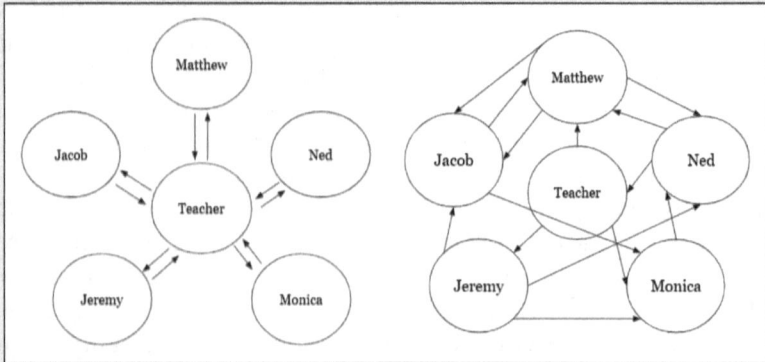

Figure 5.1. Discussion Mapping. *Courtesy of the authors*
The discussion on the left demonstrates the IRE model with the adult facilitator carrying the weight of questioning and responding. The discussion on the right demonstrates a more democratic discussion in which students direct questions and responses toward each other rather than only toward the facilitator.

Focus on Narrative Writing

At its heart, the workshop model is meant to shift ownership of learning from the teacher to the student, provide differentiated instruction based on student interests, and create collaborative communities to give feedback and celebrate success.

This means that Collaborative Reader Workshop can also serve as a template for English teachers to experiment with writing workshop. In a writing workshop model, individual students are continually drafting and revising written pieces in genres of their own choice and for purposes of their own design. In a writing workshop model, a class period usually includes a brief mini lesson about craft or genre and then long stretches of time for students to work independently, pair up for constructive feedback, or conference one-on-one with the instructor.

Nancie Atwell (2007) describes a weekly structure that combines a reader workshop approach with writing workshop: one day for book talks and self-selected reading, three days for writing workshop, and a fifth day for collaborative discussions (116). In Atwell's model, the discussion day focuses on common readings, which also serve as model texts for students' work in their writing workshop.

The benefits of writing workshop are obvious—differentiated instruction, student choice, the development of independence and problem-solving, to name a few—but it's a lot to juggle. You can't release students into this model without intensive structuring.

Collaborative Reader Workshop can provide a means to shift into writing workshop, especially once your students are familiar with the procedures and expectations. During a narrative unit, for example, you could invite students to focus on analyzing the writer's craft in their one pagers (i.e., How does the author use vivid word choice to develop imagery?).

Then during writing workshop, they can practice applying the technique in their own writing. That way, their self-selected reading becomes the mentor text. Rather than share elements they found interesting in their self-selected books, students share excerpts from their own written pieces for their small group to read, comment on, and celebrate and discuss ways to publish work for a larger audience.

DIFFERENT WAYS FOR STUDENTS TO INTERACT WITH THEIR BOOKS

Depending on your objectives and assessment, you may want to provide other ways for students to interact with and reflect on their relationships with their books. With all the added digital ways that students have to share their personal stories, why not incorporate additional ways for students to share and reflect on their personal reading journeys?

Goal Setting

Collaborative Reader Workshop relies on shared goals. While each student is reading a book that works best for their interests and their reading proficiencies, they are all working toward the same objective. One month, they may all examine how the authors create a setting in the exposition, and the next month, they may all think about how internal and external conflicts are developed throughout their self-selected narratives.

In a traditional classroom, the teacher selects the workshop focus. This makes sense, especially if you align the workshop focus with the whole-class unity of study. However, to shift more ownership onto the students, you may adapt this model so that groups of readers are selecting their own goals as a group. Perhaps you provide a list of possible choices, or if your students have demonstrated growth in their understanding of the elements of literature throughout the semester, you could remove the support at the end of the year and allow groups to select any literary element to study during their final discussion. By removing the extra scaffolding, you are preparing students to continue to find their own purposes in reading as they get ready to leave your classroom.

This adaptation also allows for a culminating project in which each Collaborative Reader Workshop group plans and teaches a lesson about their chosen literary element. Since they will be developing their lesson with evidence from a variety of texts, this final project provides an opportunity to practice synthesis as well.

One-on-One Conferences

Another instructional strategy that can easily be added to Collaborative Reader Workshop is student-teacher conferencing. Some teachers like to conference with students during daily independent reading, noting how many pages they've read and talking about their choices.

If you want to maintain the sacredness of quiet independent reading time but also want to conference with students, you might decide not to schedule yourself as a group facilitator on discussion day. While students discuss their reading in small groups, you could pull one student at a time to have a quick, individualized conversation with you. If you give your students time to write their one-pager analyses during class, you could also use that time as an opportunity for conferencing.

One-on-one conferences provide differentiated instruction that focuses on specific students' academic needs or areas of interest. A conference can be simple. Start by letting the student talk, either about what he notices in the book in general or about how that month's focus area shows up in his book. This sharing provides an initial opportunity for students to begin organizing their thoughts for their one-pager responses and receive formative feedback.

After the student talks through his analysis, pick a point of instruction and teach an individualized mini lesson. These lessons do not need to be complicated. It could be a time to push your students into thinking rhetorically about their text. For example, if a student is reading *Gone Girl*, the popular murder mystery novel by Gillian Flynn, she may identify that the narrator, Nick, who is suspected of murdering his wife, has external conflicts with the police, his sister, and his wife's parents. You probably will notice that the student has more to say about the major—and obvious—conflict between Nick and the police. So your job is to push her to consider the smaller, more subtle points of tension: Why did Flynn even give Nick a sister? Isn't there enough conflict already? How does this conflict with his sister impact Nick? Why is it there?

In these one-on-one conferences, whether the student comes up with a "right" answer to the question doesn't matter because there is no "right" answer. What matters is that you are pushing your student to think analytically about the author's purpose. You are helping them to develop a habit of mind: Good readers ask questions. Good readers consider how the small details impact the whole. Good readers think about what the author is trying to do.

Dialogue Letters

One pagers, as described in chapter 3, are an efficient way to consistently assess your students' reading analysis and writing proficiency. But they're not the only way.

In her workshop model for seventh- and eighth-grade classes, Atwell (1998) exchanges dialogue letters with her students in composition notebooks used as journals. She starts the year with a letter that describes the journal as "a place for you, me, and your friends to talk this year about books, reading, authors, and writing" (296). Students are assigned to write a page-long letter to Atwell or to a friend once a week and respond when they receive a letter.

Handwritten letters feel personal. Letter writing encourages students to reflect more thoughtfully and honestly about their reading experiences. Although high school teachers cannot commit to responding to weekly letters from a hundred students, it could be useful to exchange personal letters (or even emails) at the start and end of the semester to establish and reflect on students' individual interests and goals.

Digital Media

There are several high-interest ways to incorporate digital media into how students engage and reflect on their reading. For example, using Instagram to create photo journeys of their books and their reading can help encourage students to read. They could take selfies of where they read or where they take their books over the weekend and share these during Collaborative Reader Workshop discussions. You could even create an assessment in which students reflect on their reading habits through the visual story their photos tell.

Another high-interest strategy to encourage students to reflect on their reading and interact with other readers is podcasting. There are many interesting podcasts out there, including interview-based shows with celebrities like Dax Shepard and Joe Rogan, which many students listen to more often than they read. By creating a podcast individually or as a Collaborative Reader Workshop group, students could share what they're reading and how they are growing as readers. These could be shared with others in the class via online learning management systems.

Taking into consideration the various ways in which your students interact with all the stories in their lives (i.e., texting, talking, online browsing, snapping pictures), it makes sense to offer a wide array of ways to connect students to their books.

DIFFERENT STRUCTURES FOR DIFFERENT COURSES

Chapter 4 addresses the common concern that Collaborative Reader Workshop takes too much time away from traditional whole-class novel study. We only see these students for fifty minutes a day, but somehow, in those fifty-minute chunks, we have to make them into better readers and communicators. To put it mildly, time is of the essence.

Collaborative Reader Workshop can take up more or less time depending on how you decide to structure daily in-class reading, time to write one pagers, time for in-class conferences, and time for collaborative discussions. Monthly discussion days are consistent enough to provide an immediate purpose for students' self-selected, independent reading, but if you are taking steps toward using more self-selected books and fewer whole-class selections, you may want to consider bimonthly or even weekly meetings.

With a biweekly structure, your students could still meet with their facilitators in discussion groups once a month and the additional Collaborative Reader Workshop discussion day could be used to offer additional practice, scaffolding, or instruction between meetings. Perhaps that day becomes a writing workshop day for students to draft and revise their one-pager responses while you conference one-on-one with specific students who need more support.

Alternatively, the second meeting could be used to practice other forms of collaborative discussions, such as student-led discussions, whole-class Socratic seminars, or fishbowl discussions during which one group observes the other group's discussion and responds in a written back channel. Devoting more time to Collaborative Reader Workshop means creating additional opportunities for differentiated instruction based on students' self-selected reading choices.

If you like the idea of allowing your students to study texts based on their own interests but don't feel ready to organize a year-long program, start with a short, more intensive mini unit. In this two- or three-week unit, students read every day, engage in mini lessons on craft or literary elements, and end each week with a discussion day. If you start the year with a mini unit, you could allow your students the opportunity to determine whether they are interested in continuing to read and discuss self-selected books throughout the remainder of the year.

If your school is looking to create—or rebuild—a summer reading program, Collaborative Reader Workshop can provide a template for that work as well. While reading self-selected books, students periodically communicate with each other by posting on an online discussion board organized by thematic or skills focuses. One of their goals could be to find connections among multiple books being discussed. When the school year starts, you can assign a one pager and create a collaborative discussion or small group discussions based on their summer reading choices. An additional benefit of using Collaborative Reader Workshop to support summer reading is that it allows you to familiarize students with the class norms and expectations surrounding independent reading and Collaborative Reader Workshop in the first weeks of school.

While Collaborative Reader Workshop can be a gentle way to introduce students to the expectations and habits of mind needed to be successful in English class, educator Julie Lausé (2004) flips the script by beginning the year with a whole-class text before transitioning into students' self-selected books. During the first week, as students read the whole-class text during independent reading time, Lausé calculates her students' reading rates and determines how many pages she can expect each student to read in a week. Then she assigns deadlines for the remainder of the whole-class text based on how long it should take the slowest reader to finish. The class does not examine the content of the whole-class text until every student can be expected to have finished reading the book (25–26).

Table 5.1. Possible Collaborative Reader Workshop Structures

Time Frame	Style	Structure
Two to four weeks	Mini unit	• Give students daily/consistent reading time for books of their choice. • Organize one discussion day at the end of the week. • Assign a one pager each week. • Your unit may focus on a specific skill (i.e., to track and analyze how theme develops) or aim to develop reading habits in your students. • Create reflective journal prompts for last week and/or last discussion (i.e., How did reader workshop impact your reading? How did discussing your book with others impact your understanding of the book? Of yourself as a reader? etc.).
Semester or full year	Monthly units	• Give students daily/consistent reading time for books of their choice. • Organize one discussion day per month. • Assign a one pager per month. • Each month focuses on a specific skill (i.e., to track and analyze how theme develops). • Create reflective journal prompts for end of each semester (i.e., How did reader workshop impact your reading? How did discussing your book with others impact your understanding of the book? Of yourself as a reader? etc.). • Help students create goals for second semester (i.e., Last semester I read two books, and this semester I'd like to read three books. Last semester I read mostly young adult love stories, and this semester, I'd like to read a science fiction novel.).
	Bimonthly units	• Meeting every other week allows for more flexibility in how your time is used. Invite facilitators for one discussion day per month and then use the other week for larger collaborative discussions, student-led lesson plans, or one-on-one conferences while students have time to read or write their one pagers.
Summer reading	Independent unit	• Allow students to read any book, if curriculum allows, or allow choice of school-approved texts. • Assign regular discussion posts. • Assign one or two digital or handwritten one pagers. • Prepare students to share one pagers in a Collaborative Reader discussion day during the first or second week after returning to school.

Of course, this means that many students will finish long before the class is ready to discuss the book together. This is when Lausé introduces self-selected, independent reading. When a student finishes the whole-class book, they're not "done." They move right on to their independent reading choices.

It must be noted that this structure requires that the language of the whole-class novel is simple enough for students to comprehend without instructional support. If it makes you nervous to allow students to read a whole-class text on their own, you can modify this structure by breaking a whole-class novel into large chunks to be discussed and analyzed only after all students have completed reading the section, rather than the entire book. When a student finishes the assigned portion of the text, they can use the remainder of the week's independent reading time to begin reading the next section or they may switch back to their independent reading choice until the next chunk is assigned.

Incorporating Reading across the Content Areas

Reading in history class? Sure. But reading in science? This is where teachers of science and English alike might balk. Science teachers may wonder why English teachers can't handle their own jobs. English teachers may worry that the science teacher is going to screw it up.

Reading strategies matter, but without background knowledge in the specific content area, a reading strategy learned in an English class won't always help students comprehend a text in their science class. In *This Is Disciplinary Literacy* (2016), ReLeah Lent argues that disciplinary teachers must be responsible for teaching literacy in their content areas rather than depending on English teachers: "English teachers should not be expected to teach students how to read in every discipline any more than math teachers should be expected to teach students how to read *War and Peace*" (22).

Since independent reading correlates positively to students' overall academic achievement in all content areas (NEA 2007), it makes sense for students to read in every class. Because wide and voracious reading helps students build the schema and background knowledge to understand disciplinary texts in history, science, art, and, yes, even math, Lent recommends that teachers across the content areas give students time to read independently in class and also push them to read at home.

If your school has not yet initiated a push for reading across the disciplines, start making that push. Your students' academic achievement depends on it. And if you don't know where to start, Collaborative Reader Workshop can provide a template. History teachers might assign students to read, analyze, and discuss historical fiction or nonfiction texts. Science teachers might assign pieces from scientific nonfiction books, like Elizabeth Kolbert's *The Sixth Extinction*, the book chosen as Chicago's "One Book, One Chicago" for the 2019–2020 school year. Even math teachers might ask their students to read nonfiction pieces to "scrutinize ways that math is reported in the media or used in real-world application" (Lent 2016, 18).

Then periodically, maybe once a month or perhaps as a mini unit, students in history or science or math might get into small groups with an adult facilitator to talk about what they have been reading. In the same way that they enjoy finding out that their science teachers love novels, too, students will get a kick out of sitting down with their English teacher, in a totally different setting, and talking about *The Sixth Extinction*, especially since the student will likely be the expert in this conversation. They get a chance to teach their teacher something!

If your administration is committed to disciplinary literacy, Collaborative Reader Workshop could be adapted into a far-reaching rotating model: in English classes one month, in science the next, and in art classes after that.

Table 5.2. Collaborative Reader Workshop across Disciplines

Discipline	Possible Texts	Possible Discussion Focuses
History/ social studies	Historical fiction, historical nonfiction, current events, journals and magazine articles, historical primary documents, timelines	Interpret primary sources, consider bias, analyze contrasts and contradictions, use knowledge from the past to make sense of the present
Science	Science fiction, scientific reports, current events, journals and magazine articles	Evaluate quality and quantity of evidence, determine validity of source, question conclusions, chart or graph data and conclusions
Math	Word problems, timelines, tables, graphs, current events	Look for patterns and relationships, read for accuracy and clear mathematical reasoning, scrutinize how math is reported in media
Languages	Fiction and nonfiction narratives in content language, current events in content language	Summarize key details, determine meaning of vocabulary words in context
Art/music	Art and music reviews, graphic novels, multimodal texts, visual texts, blogs, personal communications and narratives	Analyze purpose of visual, determine whose viewpoint is being heard and whose isn't, analyze author's purpose
Special education	Content area specific texts, varied Lexile levels	Any of the previous discussion focuses based on content area and appropriate level of material

Source: Adapted from information found in Lent (2016).

Not only will students learn that all adults value literacy, but they will also discover that literacy looks different in different disciplines, a theory that will foster their growth as readers in whatever field they enter postgraduation.

Organizing Collaborative Reader Workshop at Different Levels

Although this book focuses on high school classrooms, the Collaborative Reader Workshop model can be adapted for students in grade levels from elementary to postsecondary. As is the case with reading across the disciplines, reading across levels requires careful planning with regard to the course content and objectives. The key components, however, stay the same: regular reading, regular writing, and regular discussion.

At the elementary level, teachers may use teaching assistants, parents, and older students to facilitate read-alouds of level-appropriate books and engage students in questions to help them consider what is happening in an image or who the characters are. At the postsecondary level, instructors can expect students to select additional reading in their content area and participate in discussions on online discussion boards about craft and literary elements. In composition and creative writing courses, the instructor might invite local writers, poets, and performers to facilitate small group discussions.

Table 5.3. Collaborative Reader Workshop across Grade Levels

Level	Reading	Writing	Discussion
Elementary	• Daily reading with grade-level appropriate texts • Incorporate read-alouds when applicable (example: teacher reads aloud book to class, then it is discussed in book club–style groups)	• Logging and reflecting on what they read daily or weekly • Writing to "pen pals" in other grades about their reading, if collaborating with other teachers	• Bring in parents, other teachers, principals, etc. to run book club–style discussions monthly or more frequently • Include local and public libraries too • Field trip to libraries for discussion days when/if possible • Create hands-on activities and/or question cards to focus and facilitate discussions

(continued)

Table 5.3. Continued

Level	Reading	Writing	Discussion
Middle school	• Consistent/daily independent reading	• One-pager responses • Quick writes	• Collaborate with other teachers • Bring in administrators/school staff • Connect to class/content themes • Invite parents/families
Secondary (high school)	• Consistent/daily independent reading	• One-pager responses • Quick writes	• Bring in other building faculty and staff • Connect to class/content themes • Invite parents/families
Postsecondary (college)	• Consistent reading time each day the class meets • Suggested/assigned reading time outside of class (an hour per week)	• Online discussion boards • One-pager responses adapted for level or students and/or connecting to class content	• Collaborate with other teachers • Combine with other classes • Meet for discussions outside of classroom (coffee shop on campus, library, common study space, etc.) • Invite local writers, poets, performers, and activists • Ask students to bring or invite impactful person in their lives

CLOSING THOUGHTS

To be an effective educator, you need to be flexible. With that in mind, Collaborative Reader Workshop allows for a plethora of adaptations to make this structure work for you and your students. There are ways to adapt to different grade levels, content areas, and uses of all three foundational elements (reading, writing, and discussion) that can modify the workshop to new students, courses, or ideas as you teach throughout the year(s).

Convinced? Chapter 6 provides steps to get started right away.

START PLANNING!

1. What is your course objective? What texts would help your students meet those objectives?
2. Aside from one-pager responses, what are other strategies you could use to engage your students in reading?
3. If you're not a high school English teacher, what types of reading are necessary in your content area? How do professionals in your discipline read?

Chapter Six

How to Get Started Next Week

> As a first-year teacher, Collaborative Reader Workshop was an excellent tool for connecting my students and me to the culture of the school. Through this model, students were able to discuss a love of reading with adults and role models within their community who embodied the goal of becoming lifelong readers.—Moira Quealy, high school English teacher

Implementing new ideas—especially large structures that incorporate multiple uses of your class time—can be overwhelming. You've already got a curriculum to teach and a group of students to support and many other responsibilities to navigate daily. With everything this book just threw at you, your brain is probably stuck on the question: *where do I start?*

To help jump-start your Collaborative Reader Workshop journey, this chapter breaks down next steps, resources, and points to consider.

SET UP

1. *Determine your objectives for Collaborative Reader Workshop.* Do you want students to become better readers? To practice literary analysis? To develop lifelong reading habits? Simply to enjoy English class?
2. *Decide on a structure that will work best in your course.* How much class time can you provide for independent reading? How often will your students be able to meet to talk about their independent reading books?
3. *Find a way to get books into your students' hands.* Do you have books in your classroom? Does your school library have a young adult literature collection expansive enough to support all of your students? Do your students have access to books outside of school? Which books will you book-talk first?

And if that's as far as you go this year, you will have made a huge difference in your students' reading lives already. You will have given them the authority to make a decision about their own education and an opportunity to read a book they enjoy. Reading for pleasure will make them better readers—faster and more fluent, more purposeful and engaged.

Once you get them reading, you can start planning how to encourage them to think more deeply about what they're reading through one-pager writing assignments and collaborative discussions.

BUILD

1. *Find a collaborator.* Building a community starts with one person outside of the classroom. Pair up with your school's librarian, a literacy coach, or another teacher interested in starting Collaborative Reader Workshop.
2. *Assign the one pager.* What will be the focus? Is it appropriate for your students to begin by reflecting on their reading habits, or will your classes jump into literacy skills practice right away?
3. *Plan your first workshop discussion.* When will it occur? How will you group your students? Will you invite facilitators for the first one? (Remember that it's perfectly okay to give your students time to meet in small groups without a facilitator, especially while you're still figuring out the best way to get the structure set up.)

There you have it: reading, writing, and collaborative discussion. Even without a school-wide community, these three components will give your students more purpose and agency over their learning. They have the chance to choose their own literacy content, think deeply about that content, and share their ideas through written responses and group discussions.

The final move is to expand your collaboration by inviting other members of the school community.

EXPAND

1. *Invite other readers for discussion.* Who can you rely on? Start with English teachers and academic coaches, but also consider who else may be interested in talking about books or developing stronger relationships with student readers. Coaches? Deans? Counselors? Send them an email. Discussion groups can vary depending on who joins you.
2. *Decide how your students will reflect.* How can students reflect on their growth in specific skills (academic and/or social-emotional learning)? How can they monitor this growth throughout Collaborative Reader workshop to help build evidence to support their reflections?

Above all, be patient and be flexible. It takes time to successfully implement a system like this, and what works for one teacher may not be what's best for your students. Let your students in on the process: Where do they want this to go? Who do they want to invite? What structure works best for them? Collaborative Reader Workshop is *for* your students. Do what's going to work best for them.

Part II

THE WHY

Chapter Seven

Why It Works

Academic Achievement

> I've seen firsthand how students' communication and language skills grow throughout the year. Their ability to articulate thoughts and engage in conversation about literature, connections to life, and relationships increase through their involvement in Collaborative Reader Workshop.—Jennifer Walsh, high school librarian

There's a meme going around social media. Maybe you've seen it. A smiling woman holds up a whiteboard. The text reads, "'I became a teacher so that I could help kids pass the state's standardized tests,' said no teacher ever."

When you were growing up, at some point it clicked that, hey, maybe you should become a teacher. What inspired you? Was it Mr. Kosik, your second-grade teacher who made you promise to dedicate your first published book to him? Did you want to inspire kids the way he inspired you? Or was it later, in high school, when Ms. O'Brien assigned you to act out the "play within a play" scene from *A Midsummer Night's Dream*, and you and your best friend watched scenes from *Dirty Dancing* to learn to dance? Is that when you realized English class could be fun?

It's true: standardized tests are not what inspire people to become teachers. Sure, we point our students toward resources to help them prepare. Maybe we even give them practice tests in class. We definitely remind them to get sleep the night before, eat a healthy breakfast, and bring a sweatshirt in case they get cold. But most of us also make sure our students know that it's just a test; it doesn't say anything important about who they are as students or as people.

That said, while the test score doesn't matter, it also . . . matters. Sometimes in very material ways. Test scores can determine whether students get into their first-choice universities, where schools land in *U.S. News and*

World Report's ranking, and whether schools earn federal funds. Test scores determine whether teachers earn a proficient rating from their evaluator and, in some states, whether they will receive raises that year.

Given this reality, it's kind of scary to give up valuable class time to let kids read and talk about books. How is that going to help them on the test? Can't they read at home? Do they even *want* to read? We all know what the statistics say: both teenagers and adults read less than they used to, a trend that is impacting reading ability as well as reading habits.

But this isn't new. In 2004, the National Endowment of the Arts (NEA) showed the education world that reading was at risk, finding the steepest decline in literary reading in the youngest age groups. In 2007, NEA added fuel to the fire, reporting that students who read the most for fun scored the highest on standardized reading tests (15). And even though elementary school students were reading at a higher ability than in previous years, NEA chairman Dana Gioia wrote in the report's executive summary that "all progress appears to halt as children enter their teenage years" (5).

The results are measurable: reading less means reading less well.

So if it's true that young people say they don't like to read (which has been reported time and time again) and it's true that reading leads to higher academic achievement (which has also been proven time and time again), then getting kids to *enjoy* reading, to *want* to read, to *choose* to read, will improve their test scores.

So why aren't we letting our kids read?

We ask educators this question all the time, and you're probably not surprised that the answers revolve around scores. Teachers are still afraid to give up time that could be used for test prep. And even if they know that self-selected reading is good for their students, it's difficult to know how to organize a curriculum that balances self-selected, independent reading with the familiar whole-class literature study expected by their students and administrators.

With Collaborative Reader Workshop, teachers can do both. You can follow the standards of your department's common curriculum while also giving your kids the chance to build the reading capacity needed to improve reading skills and achieve higher scores on those pesky tests. You can use the monthly one pagers to track student growth. And, most importantly, you can build student interest and buy-in through monthly book discussions.

This chapter describes how Collaborative Reader Workshop helps students to practice (and grow!) their skills in reading, writing, and speaking. If you and your administration are already sold on the usefulness of Collaborative Reader Workshop, skip ahead. But if your principal, your department chair, or your students' parents are emailing you to ask, *Where's the proof?* read on. And get those highlighters ready.

HOW COLLABORATIVE READER WORKSHOP IMPROVES READING SKILLS

Reading to Strengthen Reading Skills

Practice makes perfect. Violinists don't get good at playing violin without hundreds of hours of practice. Aspiring authors don't knock it out of the park with their first draft. Heart surgeons don't operate on their first day out of the classroom. You get the idea.

So why would reading (or reading parts of) five or six novels be enough practice for developing readers throughout the course of a whole school year? Our students keep replaying the same sad refrain, usually something like: *Well, I used to read all the time, but now I'm too busy.*

Between sports practice, homework, and Netflix binges, students are studying for AP classes, trying to build their resumes with extracurriculars, maybe working part-time jobs, and definitely trying to get more followers on social media. It's not hard to understand. Students are reading less than they used to for the same reasons adults probably read less than they did when they were younger: There's way more going on.

Like any other skill that requires practice, more practice means bigger gains, and less practice means smaller gains. Reading for pleasure leads to better reading comprehension, writing style, vocabulary, spelling, fluency, reading speed, and grammatical development, so naturally, students who don't read for pleasure have lower achievement and lower test scores.

Educator Stephen Krashen (2004) found that in thirty-eight of forty-one studies, students who were given time to read self-selected books in class "did as well or better in reading comprehension tests than students given traditional skill-based reading instruction" (2). Findings by the National Education Association (2007) back this up: "Students who read the most for fun scored the highest on standardized reading tests" (15).

And you know that STAR reading assessment that your school's reading specialist gives the students? The company that manages that test is called Renaissance, and even they insist that students who read more score higher. For them, the magic number is fifteen: their findings suggest that students who read at least fifteen minutes a day demonstrate reading gains higher than the national average.

Sure, Renaissance wants your administration to buy the STAR assessment, but that doesn't mean they're wrong about this. To do better on their test, students don't need you to purchase a fancy curriculum; they need fifteen minutes to read. Nancie Atwell captures it perfectly in *The Reading Zone* (2007): "A child sitting in a quiet room with a good book isn't a flashy or, more significantly, marketable teaching method. It just happens to be the only way for anyone ever to grow up to become a reader" (12).

Reading more doesn't only make you better at reading. Study after study demonstrates that students who read recreationally show improved proficiency in math and science, too. According to Atwell, "the top 5 percent of U.S. students read up to 144 times more than the kids in the bottom 5 percent" (107), so part of the reason that reading leads to improvement in other subjects is that reading is one of the only practical ways for students to build background knowledge about cultures, experiences, and bodies of knowledge that they wouldn't otherwise be exposed to.

Writing to Strengthen Reading Skills

Even though Atwell is correct that important learning happens when a child sits in a quiet room with a good book, Collaborative Reader Workshop also believes that a lot of important learning happens when students are pushed to think more deeply—and critically—about a question in their book.

To encourage this deep thinking, students write one-pager responses before each discussion day. Students don't write simply to prove they read. They write to learn. They write to discover. Writing is problem solving. When students write, they see relationships between thoughts—a skill that makes them into smarter, more critical thinkers (Krashen 2004, 137).

As students consider which minor character has a major impact on the plot or even why they would rate the book an eight out of ten instead of seven or nine out of ten, they are thinking—in a sustained and deep way—about the literary elements of the book. They are asking themselves questions the way practiced readers do. And, importantly, one pagers hold students accountable without destroying their reading experience.

A student can learn to fill in the right bubble on a standardized reading test without becoming a better reader. Fortunately, your students don't need to color in a single bubble to effectively practice the skills in the standards. Monthly one pagers can help teachers assess and track students' reading growth in "key ideas and details" of the Common Core Reading Standards.

Although the Common Core State Standards (CCSS) Reading Standards for key ideas are assessed in every one pager, allowing you to track student growth over time, the other reading standards on "craft and structure" and "integration of knowledge and ideas" can also be assessed throughout the year with specific one-page prompts.

For each Collaborative Reader Workshop discussion, students choose from many different one pagers—many of which are pulled from Gallagher's *Readicide* and from Kylene Beers and Robert Probst's *Notice and Note*. Table 7.1

Table 7.1. How One-Pager Prompts Align with Common Core State Standards

	CCSS Reading Standard	Prompt Ideas
Craft and structure	4. Interpret words and phrases as they are used in a text, including determining technical, connotative, and figurative meanings, and analyze how specific word choices shape meaning or tone.	*Prompt*: An author's choice of style and language can tell us a lot about the situation, the speaker, and the audience Select three to five quotes from your book so far and explain the style. Is the language formal or informal? Is it journalistic? Does it use dialect? Who does it sound like? Does it use figurative language? Then explain how the style impacts the meaning of what's being said. Consider: if the author changed the style, how would the meaning change? *Nonfiction prompt*: Same as fiction prompt.
	5. Analyze the structure of texts, including how specific sentences, paragraphs, and larger portions of the text (e.g., a section, chapter, scene, or stanza) relate to each other and the whole.	*Fiction prompt*: When the author interrupts the action to tell you about a memory, ask yourself, "Why might this be important?" The answer will tell you about the theme and conflict or will foreshadow what might happen later in the story. Then explain the significance of the memory. *Nonfiction prompt*: When the author interrupts his argument to tell an anecdote (or little story), ask yourself, "Why might this be important?" Think about a significant memory, piece of research, anecdote, etc. that the author chooses to highlight. Then explain the significance of the aside.
	6. Assess how point of view or purpose shapes the content and style of a text.	*Fiction prompt*: Sometimes characters say something they don't really mean. We call this "verbal irony" or sometimes "sarcasm." Think about a moment in the text when a character does this. Why do they say this? What do they really mean? What does this reveal about them? Then explain the significance of this moment. *Nonfiction prompt*: Sometimes writers use specific stylistic or persuasive elements, such as word choice or appeals to emotion, to add power to their point of view. Think about a moment in the text when the author uses a specific element particularly effectively. Then explain how the author uses the element to build her argument.

shows how CCSS Reading Standards 4-6 can be practiced through one-pager prompts. These prompts align with the standards while student choice maximizes students' interest in and ownership over their own thinking.

Of course, the prompts in this chapter are only examples. As you adapt Collaborative Reader Workshop for your own classroom, you will create one-pager prompts that work for you, your readers, and your departmental goals. For example, if your school assigns summer reading, you could start the year by offering students an option to write about their summer reading books as practice for the first Collaborative Reader Workshop discussion. If you teach in a school that requires specific whole-class texts, you could assign a prompt that asks students to compare their self-selected book to one of the year's whole-class texts. The point is this: your students' monthly one pagers help them practice the reading standards and help you assess their progress in reaching proficiency in these standards.

But isn't it too easy for students to practice these skills with young adult books? Your department chair is right: you probably do want your students to read texts with vocabulary and language constructions more complex than the language found in Becky Albertalli's *Simon vs. the Homo Sapiens Agenda*. But the thing about *Simon vs. the Homo Sapiens Agenda* is that teenagers love it. Which means they read it.

In *Book Love* (2013), Kittle says that we "can't have every student start with Austen, no matter what the Common Core or your department chair says. A book isn't rigorous if students aren't reading it" (xvi). Take a minute to read that again: "A book isn't rigorous if students aren't reading it." Wouldn't that make a great T-shirt? You can't start with the hard stuff.

Think of books like *Simon vs. the Homo Sapiens Agenda* as gateways to higher level reading. The National Council of Teachers of English (NCTE) states that literacy assessment includes "beliefs about literacy, dispositions toward literacy, and self-efficacy regarding literacy" (2018b). Finishing a book like *Simon*, especially for a student who doesn't see herself as a reader, helps that student feel confident in her reading abilities and ready to take on the next book.

And what a gateway *Simon* is! Not only is it a way for students to improve their reading comprehension and build stamina to tackle more complex texts, it also pushes them to think deeply about friendship and sexual identity and what it means to have a say over your own story.

Discussing to Strengthen Reading Skills

A final and important note about reading is that students' reading proficiency doesn't only improve while they're reading or writing about what they read.

Talking about books, especially with adults who love to read, models how to think while reading: how to ask useful questions, draw good conclusions, create mental images, call on background knowledge, and identify important details to support their claims.

Students also practice these skills in their one-pager responses, but without thoughtful discussion, comprehension loses relevance. The NCTE (2018b) calls literacy assessment "a social process, not a technical activity." By observing adults—and other students—using reading strategies and by discussing those strategies with them, students become both more willing and proficient readers.

Each Collaborative Reader Workshop discussion focuses on a specific literary element (i.e., characterization, theme, conflict, language, and style), so the discussion allows students to discover how authors develop literary elements for different purposes in different genres. The discussion offers an opportunity for students to make connections between multiple books. This means that they have regular practice "analyzing how two or more texts address similar themes or topics in order to build knowledge or to compare the approaches the authors take" (CCSS.R.L.9).

When a student who loves dystopian novels like *The Hunger Games* discovers that *Beartown* by Fredrik Bachman also examines the question of who has—and who doesn't have—a voice in society, that student is thinking about and discussing how an author develops theme throughout a text while also adding to his or her read-next list, a move that will offer a step into a new genre. Student surveys at the end of Collaborative Reader Workshop discussion days show that students help each other become better readers by making connections and comparing ideas across multiple texts.

In its 2018 "Call to Action" regarding literacy instruction, NCTE also reminds educators that the way a discussion is set up matters: "Conversations and discussions regarding texts must be authentic, student initiated, and teacher facilitated." In Collaborative Reader Workshop discussions, the adult is a facilitator and a participant, not the expert. Since students may always write their one pager in response to whichever prompt interests them, it's their ideas and questions—not the facilitator's—that determine the course of the discussion.

HOW COLLABORATIVE READER WORKSHOP IMPROVES WRITING SKILLS

Reading to Strengthen Writing Skills

The reading, writing, and discussion components of Collaborative Reader Workshop improve students' reading proficiency, and it turns out that better readers are also better writers. In its 2007 report, the NEA found that teenagers who read for pleasure on a daily or weekly basis scored better on reading *and* writing tests than infrequent readers (15). It makes sense. As they read book after book, readers come across a wide variety of sentence structures and grammatical constructions. When you see that authors stick commas on both sides of an appositive twenty or thirty or a hundred times, that rule starts to stick.

It matters, too, how a reader approaches a text. Research also shows that writing style develops not from writing experience, but from reading widely (Krashen 2004, 132). If students see a book as an assignment they will be tested on, they won't read to enjoy the author's craft. Rather, they will home in on key plot points and characters, doing their best to memorize the specific details that will prove that they read it—even if what they read was the SparkNotes guide.

When they're used to daily independent reading, however, students are more likely to see books as a source of entertainment—something to do for pleasure. Then at the end of the month, when they are asked to look deeper at whatever book they're currently reading, they will reread for a different purpose: to analyze the development or purpose of a literary element (and to support their claims with textual evidence). Practicing multiple ways of reading helps students practice the critical thinking skills that foster more effective reading *and* writing.

Writing to Strengthen Writing Skills

You probably don't have to be convinced that writing more frequently helps students become better writers. So here's what we like about one pagers, an idea we adapted from Gallagher's *Readicide* (2009): one pagers make for *consistent* and *nonthreatening* writing practice. They're not scary.

Regardless of whatever else is happening in your classroom—narrative writing to practice for college essays? research for debates? poetry analysis? grammar review?—you and your students know that once a month, they will be expected to write a page of analysis about their self-selected books. Since each student chooses the book and the writing prompt, they feel more interest in the assignment, and when they're more interested, they're more invested in doing well, which leads to more genuine practice.

Regular practice also means regular feedback on the writing skills they need to master: focus, organization, and language. One pagers also require students to use and incorporate evidence in their writing (CCSS.W.9), but to avoid penalizing students too heavily, the use of evidence is assessed on the reading side of the rubric.

The rubric never changes, so if you teach in a school that requires evidence of growth over time, the writing (and reading) scores are easily tracked. This makes it easy to prove that a student who wasn't smoothly incorporating evidence at all in September consistently incorporates it with quote introductions by November—but perhaps still needs to work on using colons correctly.

In *Readicide*, Gallagher describes using one-pagers as "jumping-off points for having book conferences with students" (83). Since one pagers can be assigned in preparation for Collaborative Reader Workshop discussion days, this is another function of the one pager: to give students a place to start in their discussions. If they completed their one pagers, they have already thought deeply about their books and have something to contribute.

Speaking to Strengthen Writing Skills

Although collaborative reader discussions are primarily meant to foster a sense of community in the classroom, these discussions also improve students' writing in two important ways. First, a student's discussion group becomes an authentic audience, a way to "publish" their writing. This means they may approach the assignment differently than a piece that they know only their English teacher will ever see.

And second, although the discussions offer a way to think about effective reading strategies (i.e., How do good readers think about what they read?), the same goes for writing skills. As students listen to other students read a few lines from their one pagers, they hear the way other inexperienced writers use language or organize their ideas. As students process their ideas aloud—and other readers build on those ideas—they develop their claims more effectively than they would on their own with their book. (They can even handwrite marginalia on their one pagers.)

Ideally, one pagers are written (and printed) before students come to discussion, but for struggling writers, Collaborative Reader Workshop discussion provides differentiated support. Not all students need to discuss their ideas aloud to develop or organize them, but for students who are stuck, the discussion process is an additional aid to help their writing process.

HOW COLLABORATIVE READER WORKSHOP IMPROVES SPEAKING AND LISTENING SKILLS

Finally, although the purpose of workshop discussion is to facilitate deeper reading and provide an authentic audience for students' ideas, it also provides a regular opportunity for students to flex their speaking and listening muscles.

Students become better readers by reading, better writers by writing, and better speakers (and listeners) by participating in collaborative discussions.

When researchers look at how high school classrooms are traditionally run, they find that students aren't talking enough. On average, 75 percent of class time is spent on instruction, and 70 percent of classroom "talk" is the teacher talking at the students (Goodlad 2004, 229). Students themselves are only engaged in discussion for 150 minutes of the seven-hour school day. This is a problem since we also know that "discussion-based approaches to academic literacy content are strongly linked to student achievement" (NCTE 2018a).

Class discussions are a strange form of communication: twenty-five people in a room, all talking about the same topic (usually decided by the teacher), all expected to have something to say, to listen, and to not interrupt. Collaborative Reader Workshop discussions try to break this formula by creating a context that approximates a real-life conversation, one that happens during a book club, for example, or spontaneously after a friend just finished a book she loved. Each reader comes to his small group with something to say, and since most of the time each reader is coming with a different book, everyone has expert knowledge that can be shared.

The adults in the group are readers, too. Collaborative Reader Workshop asks adult facilitators to avoid the traditional, teacher-centered pattern in which a teacher asks a question, a student responds, and then the teacher responds to the student's response. Instead, this is a conversation—one that requires that students come prepared with evidence, ask effective questions, and respond to other participants. The facilitator's job is to nudge students to articulate their ideas clearly and deeply, making sure speakers have enough wait time and encouraging them to say more.

Although these skills aren't formally assessed, regular practice still improves our students' collaborative discussion skills. The Common Core State Standards for Speaking and Listening notes that students should participate in a variety of collaborative discussions. Table 7.2 explains how students practice each standard during Collaborative Reader Workshop discussions.

There's no need to formally assess speaking and listening skills during workshop discussion days. Most English classes consist of plenty of fishbowl discussions, literary circles, and Socratic seminars that provide opportunities for teachers to give students feedback and, sometimes, a grade. It's more important to make Collaborative Reader Workshop discussions as authentic as possible. A grade would kill that.

Finally, Collaborative Reader workshop is about joy, about connecting readers in a positive, encouraging environment. As readers get older, they often lose their love of school at the same time as their love of books.

Table 7.2. Common Core State Standards for Speaking and Listening

CCSS Speaking and Listening Standard	How Readers Practice the Standard
1.A. Come to discussions prepared, having read and researched material under study; explicitly draw on that preparation by referring to evidence from texts and other research on the topic or issue to stimulate a thoughtful, well-reasoned exchange of ideas.	Students come to Collaborative Reader Workshop meetings after a month of daily reading with a one pager that explores a literary topic in their book. They know the one pager will give them ammunition for the discussion.
1.B. Work with peers to promote civil, democratic discussions and decision-making, set clear goals and deadlines, and establish individual roles as needed.	At the start of the semester, when Collaborative Reader Workshops are formed, students discuss and determine norms to facilitate a successful discussion. Teachers may ask students to establish individual roles, especially in lieu of adult facilitators. (See chapter 5 for adaptations.)
1.C. Propel conversations by posing and responding to questions that probe reasoning and evidence; ensure a hearing for a full range of positions on a topic or issue; clarify, verify, or challenge ideas and conclusions; and promote divergent and creative perspectives.	During Collaborative Reader Workshop discussions, students practice listening and asking meaningful questions. Facilitators model this behavior as well.

By creating a different environment and refocusing their energies in a hands-on way, even for a day, we help students reframe how they see literacy and school as a whole. We want our students to enjoy talking about the books they love and to learn about new books to try. Nancie Atwell (2007) encourages teachers to pay attention to the reading "experts" in our rooms (32). You may not read a lot of fantasy books, but one of the readers in your room probably does, and he can teach the other readers in his discussion about the genre and make recommendations for future reads.

CLOSING THOUGHTS

We want you to trust us: Collaborative Reader Workshop works. We hope this chapter proves why. A student won't get better at reading or writing or speaking by answering a single question during a teacher-run class discussion about a book they partially read, and they definitely won't learn to read or write by filling in bubbles to prove they read.

Students only get better at reading by reading—and then by writing and talking and thinking about what they read. They only get better at writing by writing and by reading models of successful writing. And they only get better at speaking in discussions by speaking in discussions.

In short, it takes practice. And students willingly practice when they find the practice interesting: when they're choosing what they read and what they write about to think more deeply about that reading These are the same skills that students practice with complex, whole-class texts. Think of it that way: Collaborative Reader Workshop isn't replacing anything. It's more practice. And we all know our students need it.

We haven't missed our chance to make readers out of our students. Students will read. Ours do.

START PLANNING!

1. What literacy skills are the highest priority in your department? In your classroom?
2. How do you currently make sure your students are becoming better readers, writers, and collaborators? What works? What would you like to change?
3. How does your school approach test preparation? How can you make that practice more meaningful?

Chapter Eight

Why It Works

Social-Emotional Learning

> Reader workshops provide staff and students with the unique opportunity to connect through books. I learn so much about students from the books they read and their reasoning behind their choice. Subsequently, they learn about me and my interests, and we each walk away from the experience with a deeper understanding of one another.—Sarah Kirkorsky, high school psychologist

All learning is social and emotional. Every interaction you have with a student impacts their social and emotional development—whether or not you're thinking intentionally about this development. Yet many educators still think of social-emotional learning (SEL) as one of those education buzzwords that sounds awesome in theory but is impossible to quantify and teach in daily practice.

Educators who believe in teaching SEL believe that students' social and emotional skills—such as self-awareness and social awareness—should grow as much as their academic skills throughout the school year. This means, too, that SEL skills should be regularly assessed so that necessary supports can be put into place for students who struggle.

This may seem obvious. Of course we want our students to learn to set their own goals and manage their emotions! In a 2017 research survey, 98 percent of school principals surveyed stated that their students would benefit from learning social-emotional skills (DePaoli, Atwell, and Bridgeland 2017). But because it's difficult to track SEL skills with numerical data, classroom teachers often see it as the responsibility of social workers or counselors. Since teachers already have enough to teach and measure in their content area, SEL gets put on the back burner much of the time.

Except in Collaborative Reader Workshop.

It's clear that Collaborative Reader Workshop makes readers into better students, but what teachers may not realize is that it also makes readers into healthier humans. Seriously.

The Collaborative for Academic, Social, and Emotional Learning (CASEL) identifies and defines five specific social-emotional competencies that students—and everyone else—should be working toward:

- Self-awareness
- Self-management
- Responsible decision-making
- Social awareness
- Relationship skills

This chapter explores how Collaborative Reader Workshop provides repeated opportunities for students to practice these competencies and reflect on their own growth in social-emotional learning.

Table 8.1. Social-Emotional Learning Competencies in Collaborative Reader Workshop

Workshop Component	Self-Awareness	Self-Management	Responsible Decision Making	Social Awareness	Relationship Skills
Daily reading	✓	✓	✓	✓	
Book talks	✓	✓			
One pagers	✓	✓	✓		
Discussion	✓	✓	✓	✓	✓

SELF-AWARENESS

Daily self-selected reading creates a pause in the day. Like us, our students deal with a lot: breakups, family stress, finding jobs, and drama in their friend groups. And that's on top of homework, upcoming tests, missing work, and college applications.

Both struggling and proficient readers benefit from setting aside the anxiety of regular schoolwork to read a pleasurable story they're interested in. A quiet space promotes calmness in the mind. Creating a space in the day for students to decompress—and modeling the choice to shut off technology—helps students to develop their own strategies for managing stress and controlling impulses. Will they slip up and take out their cell phones from time to time? Sure. So, without scolding or judgment, remind them to focus on the task at hand. As you consistently encourage them to control their impulses, they will build this competency.

Setting explicit and thoughtful guidelines for daily reading, as discussed in chapter 1, builds a positive space for students to understand and make appropriate choices about their own behavior and social interactions. It takes some time to reiterate the purpose of reading guidelines—such as keeping the room quiet, storing technology out of sight, and ensuring music isn't too loud in their headphones—but explaining the purpose behind these rules challenges students to evaluate their own behavior and how it impacts their environment and those around them.

You can also help students recognize when they're struggling with a text through one-on-one check-ins. If a student reads only difficult books that he needs to stretch to understand, then he will not enjoy reading and will not develop a habit since "there's no pleasure in constant confusion" (Kittle 2013, 5). If a student has only read ten pages this week, don't assume that she is simply choosing not to focus or deliberately disobeying your instruction. Instead, ask her to consider why her pace has slowed down. Is she still interested in her book? Is it too challenging? Is it time to try something new? Or maybe there's something blowing up on her phone. Does she want you to hold on to it during reading?

Posing these questions for your students helps them notice their own feelings and offers a strategy to use on their own. In its "Statement on Independent Reading," the National Council of Teachers of English (NCTE) confirms the goal of independent reading: "to build habitual readers with conscious reading identities" (2019). When students decide to give up a book and try something new, don't roll your eyes at their impatience. Help them to understand why they're making that choice and praise their self-awareness. Help them establish the reading habits they'll use outside of your classroom. And yes, sometimes adult readers choose to stop reading a book that's boring them.

Choice intrinsically breeds self-awareness. Having choice about which books they read and which one-pager prompts they write about also pushes students to become more self-aware about their interests and skills. In most classes, the instructor decides what students read and write about, so choice is sometimes a new experience for students. In order to decide whether to analyze the significance of a minor character or identify internal and external conflicts or write an additional chapter of the book, students need to be self-aware: What is their reading of the text? How can they effectively demonstrate this understanding?

Similarly, as students self-reflect and receive feedback on their one-pager responses, they are better able to assess their strengths and limitations as writers and readers. Throughout the year (or semester) students will look back at your feedback on their writing, set goals, and improve their work for the next discussion day. Recognizing their personal growth as readers and writers alongside consistent one-pager guidelines helps students to develop a sense of confidence and a growth mindset.

Students also develop an idea of who they are as a speaker and a listener through Collaborative Reader Workshop in a different way than they may have with previous classroom discussions. In many collaborative discussions, students fear not knowing the right answer or feel anxious about whether they have spoken enough to earn points, but on Collaborative Reader Workshop days, there is no right answer and there are no points. These small group discussions allow students to become comfortable (or at least familiar) with the people they're talking to and the books they're discussing. In their post-discussion reflections, students will also consider how they learn and communicate with others.

STUDENT STORY: EVIE BREAKS OUT OF HER SHELL

Evie was a quiet girl in a class of rambunctious boys. She was extremely soft spoken and experienced challenges at home, which Mrs. Fleck wouldn't know about until Evie shared them with her the next year when Mrs. Fleck was no longer her teacher.

And yet, in Collaborative Reader Workshop, Evie transformed from believing that she wasn't a talker to seeing herself as an important—and beloved—member of the classroom community. She had forgotten her childhood love for reading until she found books like *Looking for Alaska* and *Eleanor & Park*, which she excitedly book-talked to the group.

Some of the same rambunctious boys who were throwing books across the room earlier that year actively listened as Evie talked about the conflicts among characters in her book. She was able—starting with small, general comments about the plot of her book at first before feeling comfortable engaging in book talks later—to increase her self-confidence as a speaker and develop a more accurate perception of herself as the avid reader and charismatic speaker she was.

SELF-MANAGEMENT

As students become more aware of their strengths, emotions, and behaviors, they can also learn to regulate their emotions and behaviors and work toward both academic and SEL goals. Collaborative Reader Workshop provides a consistent routine with consistent expectations, and this reliability—lasting throughout the school year or semester—allows students to reflect on previous behavior and accomplishments, set goals, and work toward achieving those goals.

If, for instance, a student starts the year without completing one pagers at all, his goal might be to simply complete the assignment. Another student might have completed the one pager hurriedly the day it was due, and her goal becomes both personal (time management) and academic (to further develop her ideas). A third student may have successfully completed his one-pager responses but wants to practice adding more specific evidence with proper Modern Language Association citations.

The motivation and goals vary from student to student, but all three will have consistent practice as well as regular opportunities to reflect on their progress and set new goals. Each one-pager prompt reminds students to reflect on their individual goals, which also allows you the opportunity to give differentiated feedback in response to those goals. Students know that these goals can be academic (e.g., about their writing or participation in discussion) or about their SEL competencies (e.g., about keeping their phones in their bags or organizing themselves to have their one-pager response complete in time for discussion day).

As students create their own goals and work toward them, they also practice self-discipline for more authentic reasons than just a grade. Students who lack self-regulation are more likely to face punitive discipline, such as being sent to the dean or suspended. As a consequence, those students are unable to learn at the same pace as their peers. Collaborative Reader Workshop is a way to maintain equity in the classroom by helping all students to develop a sense of agency.

STUDENT STORY: BILL MEETS CALVIN AND HOBBES

Bill had attention deficit hyperactivity disorder. He struggled with controlling his impulses and focusing during daily reading. He regularly took out his cell phone and played music (sometimes very loudly) during reading time. He sometimes got up and crossed the room to talk to his friends, taking away from their reading time, too.

Ms. Heinemann had many conversations with Bill about the purpose of reading. She reminded him that this was a time to de-stress and pointed out the negative impact he was having on his own reading and his peers' experiences.

It took time. Eventually, though, Bill discovered Calvin and Hobbes. Although Bill could have been reading books with much higher Lexile scores, *Calvin and Hobbes* was what Bill needed at the time. He was able to focus for the daily ten minutes of reading. Now outbursts occurred only when he chuckled at something in one of the comics.

Even though Bill didn't master control of all of his impulses and still gave in to distractions sometimes, the consistency of daily reading time gave him the opportunity to find a text he enjoyed and to work toward goals of self-management and responsible decision making. He also saw growth, recognizing that self-management continued to be a struggle for him but that he was less of a distraction to himself and others.

RESPONSIBLE DECISION-MAKING

In a traditional English classroom structure, decision making is often limited to what's outlined in the department or district curriculum. If anyone in the classroom gets to contribute to decision making, it's the teacher who decides when the students will listen, when they will talk, and what they read and talk about.

Of course, teachers have the expertise to make constructive decisions to help students grow, but this reality also means that, in many classrooms, the only decision students get to make is whether they do the work or not. When they choose not to do the work, they are corrected swiftly without time to reflect on their choices. This is detrimental to students' ability to analyze situations, identify problems, and reflect on their own participation and growth.

As explained in the previous section, Collaborative Reader Workshop provides consistent opportunities for students to evaluate their own engagement and proficiency and set goals for the future. Sometimes this means that they learn to identify problems: Are they not marking due dates in their planner? Are they sticking with a book that doesn't interest them? Are they not setting aside time to read and write at home? Are they not prepared to speak up in their discussions? To meet their individual goals, students need to evaluate and reflect on their own behavior.

When students are told to think about an inappropriate choice they made and reflect on it after the fact, they connect reflection with discipline and, sometimes, punishment. Instead of a skill that all healthy humans practice, reflection becomes something you do when an adult is upset with you. However, if students are regularly prompted to reflect on the choices they are making—regarding their participation, engagement, and academic practice—they learn to identify their own purposes for responsible decision making.

By participating in Collaborative Reader Workshop, students also learn to make responsible decisions regarding what they read and write. In the traditional English classroom, not only do teachers choose all the texts that are studied, they also choose how the students should be responding to these texts. Literary analysis prompts, for example, often ask students to use evidence from the text to support a predetermined reading of a predetermined text. As Atwell (1998) notes, using only whole-class texts inadvertently teaches students that "there is one interpretation of a text: the teacher's (or the teacher manual's)" (28–29). The decisions are made for them.

Giving students choices about how they approach a text—as well as opportunities to discuss various interpretations of that text—gives students agency over their own ethical decision making instead of creating a game of rule following to please the teacher.

STUDENT STORY: CECE FINDS A SPARK

Cece, a sophomore English student, wanted to be an elementary teacher someday—but never wanted to do work in class.

When Mrs. Fleck gave Cece the opportunity to reflect on how she was growing as a reader and writer, she wrote at first that she just didn't like reading *or* writing. According to those early reflections, she could not grow these skills because she did not enjoy practicing them.

After regular reading, discussions, and reflection prompts, however, Cece discovered something that did motivate her: her goal to become a teacher. She made the decision to spend a Collaborative Reader Workshop cycle reading and writing about books she thought her students might one day read. When she realized she was allowed to read children's literature and analyze these texts for what her future students could learn, she was more invested in the work personally and noticed that "reading books that make me think about my future helps me learn and think about how to help my future students learn too."

This built-in reflection gave Cece the chance to analyze her situation, identify the problem, and then solve it. If Cece had instead been required to read whole-class texts to answer a question her teacher decided was important, she may not have reflected on the personal connection she has to children's literature and the future decisions she is hoping to make in her own classroom.

SOCIAL AWARENESS

It's no secret that reading stories about people, worlds, cultures, and issues that are outside of our own bubble helps build social awareness. American students who know Trevor Noah only from television and have no idea about his background can read about apartheid and South African culture in *Born a Crime*. Students who know nothing about the emotional manipulation and trauma of sex trafficking can take the perspective of a teenage girl who experiences this world in *Dime* by E. R. Frank.

Students who already call themselves readers can use daily self-selected reading to challenge themselves to learn about other subjects, like health and science in *Why Zebras Don't Have Ulcers* or climate change in *The Sixth Extinction*. Since students can count on daily reading time and know that it's okay to try a book and then abandon it, they feel more comfortable picking books and genres that challenge their own knowledge, preferences, and views. This experience allows them to see different perspectives that they may not encounter in their daily lives in- or outside of school.

When young readers step into someone else's shoes by reading about experiences outside of their own, they build empathy. For example, *Some As-*

sembly Required, Arin Andrews's memoir about being a transgender young adult, gives cis students a low-stakes opportunity to learn more about challenges in the trans community. Reymundo Sanchez's books, *My Bloody Life*, *Once a King Always a King*, and *Lady Q*, show why young people may join gangs. *Wonder* by R. J. Palacio about a child with Treacher Collins syndrome, *I Am Not Your Perfect Mexican Daughter* by Erika Sanchez about a Mexican American teenager mourning her sister's death, and *Between the World and Me* by Ta-Nehisi Coates about the realities of being a black man in America explore diverse themes and encourage students to share their own. Experiencing diverse perspectives helps students increase their respect for others.

> **TEACHER TIP: DIVERSIFY YOUR CLASSROOM LIBRARY**
>
> Although we ask facilitators to bring a book to talk about to each Collaborative Reader Workshop discussion day, Gisele Ramilo, English teacher and social-emotional learning coach at Oak Park and River Forest High School, a diverse Chicagoland high school, always brings a stack of four or five books by diverse authors. She often hands these books to the students in her group or leaves them with the classroom teacher afterward.
>
> To build empathy in your young readers, access to diverse perspectives is key. "Assuming the classroom library is diverse in genres, time periods, and authors, students also have an enriching experience of choosing books they might not have ever read if not for the Reader Workshop," Ramilo reminds us. "They might, on a whim, pick up a dystopian novel by a female author, a science fiction text by a contemporary writer, or a memoir by a writer of color. All these potential reading experiences seek to create empathy in our young readers and enlighten their minds into the multiplicity of differences and thinking that exists."

As a workshop facilitator and daily reader in your classroom, diversifying your own reading is key to building SEL skills—specifically social awareness and relationship building. Think of all the different kinds of students you have in your classroom and your school, including students in the LGBTQ community, students with disabilities or mental health issues, students of various races, religions, and so on. Reading and book-talking both fiction and nonfiction texts that align with the diversity in your own classroom helps foster your own social awareness, which makes you a more effective educator as you help your students build respect for others and appreciate diverse perspectives. Your own wide reading also helps you make recommendations for specific students who need a better understanding of specific groups.

STUDENT STORY: ANTONIO SEES HIS STORY IN A BOOK

Antonio was a wonderfully creative and bright human being struggling with his identity. He shared with Mrs. Fleck, who was his teacher for junior and senior year, that he hadn't come to terms with his sexuality and mental health issues.

Antonio and Mrs. Fleck connected through books his junior year when she gave him tons of suggestions and he started to find stories he loved. By senior year, he was the one giving her recommendations. Instead of reading what was on her read-next list or a book assigned for her graduate program, Mrs. Fleck picked up *Aristotle and Dante Discover the Secrets of the Universe* by Benjamin Alire Sáenz based on Antonio's recommendation.

Without even realizing that the book was about a teenager struggling with his sexuality, working to control his anger, and trying to balance his Mexican and American identities (and feeling that he wasn't enough of either), Mrs. Fleck immediately fell in love with the story. After daily reading, she and Antonio gushed about the novel often enough that other students—completely different from the characters depicted in the book—picked it up for their next read as well.

Taking Antonio's suggestion helped Mrs. Fleck build an even stronger relationship with him and validated Antonio's experiences and struggles.

Good readers enjoy this privilege of understanding the outlook of others. Perhaps because of this active empathy, they contribute in measurable ways to civic and social improvements (NEA 2007, 90). These diverse perspectives help readers see the world differently, and once they see the world differently, they may choose to live differently, too.

RELATIONSHIP SKILLS

Although reading widely helps students to build empathy and social awareness, Collaborative Reader Workshop discussions help them apply those new understandings and practice relationship skills. Given all the distractions of the modern world, students can sometimes struggle with truly listening to others—their interests, ideas, and emotions. In its "Call to Action," the NCTE insists that "conversations and discussions regarding texts must be authentic, student initiated, and teacher facilitated" (2018a). Collaborative Reader Workshop discussions set aside time and space for students to practice authentic communication and listening about texts and topics raised by other students.

Talking about diverse characters or situations in a book also opens the door for students to share their own personal challenges or questions that align with what they're reading. This sharing builds relationships and forms community, giving students a reason to engage in discussion.

You can also be deliberate about giving students a reason to build relationships and practice teamwork. For example, if you start or end a Collaborative Reader Workshop discussion day by prompting the groups to make a top-five books list (e.g., top scary stories, top book-to-movie picks, top books to read before you graduate, etc.), this activity pushes them to create together as they evaluate which books should be on each list. They have a common goal to work toward and build relationships with each other through this work. The teacher may facilitate this discussion and help redirect to the specific lists, but the students run the activity and fuel the collaborative decision-making.

Even when the discussions veer away from books, students gain from interacting with students and staff that they otherwise wouldn't talk to. Educator Steven Wolk (2008) puts it another way: "Schools need to find ways for students, teachers, and administrators to take a break from the sometimes emotional, tense, and serious school day and have some fun together."

Students learn better when they take mindful pauses to process information and give their brains a break. Discussion day gives students a chance to share their reading and writing and reflect on their growth, but, maybe more importantly, these discussions are a break from the normal school day. And, as your students will tell you, they're fun.

STUDENT STORY: WINSTON TURNS COMMUNITY LEADER

When Ms. Heinemann first met Winston, he was a quiet kid who said he never liked reading. Two years later, as a graduating senior, Winston cited reader workshop as the reason he met new friends: "I didn't know a lot of people in my class, maybe two or three, then at the end of the year I kinda knew everybody." He went on to say he liked "talking to people about books and meeting new teachers."

Without this structure, Winston would have continued to be the quiet kid in the back of the room who struggled with homework completion. Instead, he felt part of a reader community, read all eight hundred–plus pages of Stephen King's *11/22/63*, and told his group members and facilitators all about it.

Shortly thereafter, *11/22/63* became a Hulu series, and based on Winston's recommendation, one of his group members decided to watch it. For the rest of the semester, they used part of their workshop discussions to excitedly react to the show and, with Winston's help, consider the director's choices in adapting it for the screen.

BRINGING IT ALL TOGETHER: COMMUNITY CREATES HEALTHIER SELVES

Being part of a community—any community—meets fundamental social-emotional needs. The third tier of Maslow's hierarchy of needs is "belonging and love." To belong is to feel accepted, to trust the other members of your tribe. Readers in Collaborative Reader Workshop get to know each other's interests and struggles—in both books and life.

This is why it's okay if the discussion veers away from books into movies or weekend plans, because one of the goals is to create a space where students can speak to each other and to adults on equal footing, developing their relationship skills and self-management. The trust and joy that comes from belonging to a community is, frankly, what keeps some students coming to school.

To develop empathy, it's not only important for students to experience other perspectives *while* reading; students also need to hear about other readers' perspectives and interests *after* reading. NCTE states that authentic, teacher-facilitated conversations about a text "should lead to diverse interpretations" (2018a). And the nature of the discussion—the fact that students interact with each other and with their faculty facilitator in a way that gives everyone relatively equal status—develops their relationship skills.

Collaborative Reader Workshop takes a purposeful step away from the traditional authority-led classroom, allowing all students to feel included in the school community. As students, especially students who do not often feel seen in the educational environment, get to know their adult facilitators, they build trust that allows for further communication. Atwell (2007) explains that teachers want their students to "get that the teacher loves books, and that our advice about reading them is trustworthy" (93). She uses the metaphor of the kitchen table: an effective classroom is like a huge dining-room table, one with enough room for every student to pull up a chair and feel included. Collaborative Reader Workshop is a way to build that table.

Or, with all due respect to Atwell, you could see Collaborative Reader Workshop as a way of destroying that table and encouraging your students to create a new one from their own lived experiences. In Collaborative Reader Workshop, it's their voices and stories, not the teacher's, that construct the table. And when you create a space for this freedom, you open yourself to the joy that comes with personal connection and storytelling. Collaborative Reader Workshop is a way of humanizing all readers, adults and adolescents alike.

CLOSING THOUGHTS

Some teachers prioritize subject-matter content over all else, including relationship building, habits of mind, and the social-emotional well-being of the students in their rooms. Ironically, though, students who feel emotionally disconnected in the academic space often have a more difficult time mastering the subject matter being prioritized.

With Collaborative Reader Workshop, you are building a community. You're offering structures for your students to actively reflect on whom they are as readers, writers, and people as they prepare for and participate in discussion. Most importantly, you're creating a safe, caring space for the young people in your room to learn to be vulnerable because they know they won't be judged.

A classroom is made up of individuals with full lives, struggles, and passions outside of school. Give them opportunities to make connections with others and share their stories.

START PLANNING!

1. How can you learn more about your students' overall social-emotional wellness?
2. What team-building opportunities can you add into your classroom/workshop?
3. When can you build in some time to discuss and reflect on social-emotional skills in your class?

Chapter Nine

Why It Works
Equity

> The traditional English curricular experience has the teacher choose a common text for all students, and quite often, the teacher is also guiding students toward meaning making and inferential thinking. Collaborative Reader Workshop, however, flips this conventional script and is essentially equity in action; students take ownership of reading by choosing their own books and constructing their own meaning from the texts they choose. Students can choose what to think about and how to think about it in the simple act of choosing their own reading. This is equity. —Gisele Ramilo, high school English teacher and social-emotional learning coach

Teachers are often told to keep politics out of education. But when people say that the teaching of literacy is inherently political, they're not wrong. If politics concerns who has—and who doesn't have—power, then the content teachers choose to teach, the books they assign, and the strategies they use during lessons are all inherently political. Even the classroom decor has political implications. When you hang images of the Founding Fathers on your classroom walls instead of a photo of Frederick Douglass, Sojourner Truth, or Malcolm X, you are making a political statement about who you see and who you don't see as an intellectual leader.

But there are only so many minutes in the day and so many days in the school year. That means some voices are heard in the classroom and some aren't. Even if a teacher is conscious about including diverse perspectives in whole-class selections, it isn't possible for a whole-class curriculum to be representative of all identities and perspectives.

Since it's not possible to include representation of every identity in the whole-class curriculum, teachers need to figure out other ways to foster equity in the classroom. In *Teaching as a Subversive Activity* (1969), Neal Postman argues that the medium is a message. If the teacher is the only source of information in the room—the only one to choose what is read and discussed—students learn that the teacher's identity and values matter more than the students' identities and values. To be an effective teacher, you need to be aware of how your background and home culture shows up in your practice.

Collaborative Reader Workshop allows for more diverse perspectives to be heard—both in the texts being studied and the way the classroom is run. By book-talking a variety of books and allowing students to choose what they want to read, you can differentiate how students practice literacy and allow students to have more of a voice in their own education. Further, when students are invited to sit alongside peers and adults and have equal say over the topic of discussion, the student's interests and curiosities are just as important as the adult's.

Of course, as the classroom teacher, you retain the power to determine the structure, pace, and frequency of Collaborative Reader Workshop, but when you let students decide what to read and what to talk about, you are shifting some of the power structure from teacher-centered to student-centered. This allows readers of all backgrounds to see themselves in the literature they study and enables students at all proficiency levels to work at a pace that supports their growth as readers, writers, and speakers. In short, this is equity work.

This chapter considers how Collaborative Reader Workshop works toward equity by allowing for differentiation and by being racially and culturally responsive.

DIFFERENTIATION THROUGH COLLABORATIVE READER WORKSHOP

In *Book Love* (2013), Penny Kittle warns us that it's "self-defeating to give all our students the same work" (4). Teachers know this: they learn about differentiation in their preservice training and explicitly plan for differentiation in the pre-observation lesson plans they turn in to their department chairs.

But with thirty—or more!—students in a classroom, it's not always easy. Differentiation usually happens through extended time, additional supports, and written feedback. Sometimes teachers can differentiate by carefully curating small groups based on need, allowing for students to work at their own paces in stations or offering a few options for assignments. It feels much more difficult, though, to differentiate through different texts. After all, to align with the expectations of the traditional English classroom, wouldn't that mean creating specific lesson plans and assessments for many different texts?

> *differentiate* (verb): to provide a range of different avenues for understanding new information and developing teaching materials and assessment measures so that all students in a diverse classroom community can learn effectively, regardless of differences in ability

Collaborative Reader Workshop provides an alternative. When all students have the chance to choose what they read, to read at individualized paces, and to select writing prompts from a range of assessment options, that means that all students—from high achieving readers to struggling readers—have the same opportunity to practice literacy skills at a level that works for them.

Rather than being separated from other students and placed in drill-and-kill remediation programs with less access to reading material that interests them, students with learning disabilities, students who don't speak English at home, and students who struggle with anxiety or attention deficit hyperactivity disorder (ADHD) all participate in Collaborative Reader Workshop. The instruction is inherently differentiated for their individual needs. Nancie Atwell (2007) says it best: "Strong readers *and* struggling readers want to know the joys and sorrows of other lives, the common dreams that unite us, and the satisfactions of great stories" (48). In Collaborative Reader Workshop, students reading at all levels get this chance.

How to Differentiate

Differentiation is built into self-selected, independent reading. Students select material that interests them and read at their own pace. Since reading rates differ with more complicated texts, it can be useful to teach your students to calculate their reading rates. How much did they read during today's ten minutes of daily reading? Multiply that by six to get an idea of how much they might read in an hour.

If you assign self-selected reading as homework (or simply encourage your students to keep reading at home), calculating reading rates can be used to ensure differentiation. All students are reading, but more advanced readers may be reading a more demanding text or finishing more pages in a week.

For example, if Elliot, a strong reader, has chosen *Pride and Prejudice* as his self-selected book, fifteen pages an hour may be an appropriate expectation for his weekly reading even though Matt, who's reading a graphic novel about Superman, is reading more than a hundred pages in an hour. Though these two students aren't expected to read an equal number of pages, they are expected to read an amount that's fair for each of them. This contrasts with whole-class reading assignments that usually require all students to finish chunks of a text at the same time.

There's differentiation in the one-pager assignment, too. Prior to Collaborative Reader Workshop discussion days, students choose how to demonstrate their reading comprehension and writing proficiency from a range of options. They select the one-pager prompt that appeals to their current interests, and you can guide specific students toward prompts that align with the practice they need.

Differentiated instructional support depends on both a student's ability to read the text and your goals for a particular text. Since the primary goal for Collaborative Reader Workshop is to create willing, lifelong readers, students' self-selected books almost always require less support than the texts chosen as whole-class reads, which align with more specific literacy goals. You may encourage students to choose texts that challenge them, but you also want them to enjoy what they've chosen, and no one enjoys a text that is too hard to read.

Regardless of reading level, students practice literacy skills in their one pagers. As detailed in chapter 2, ask your students to write brief reflections at the bottom of their one pagers to consider what skills—both literacy and executive functioning skills—they practiced that month. These reflections prompt you to give each student differentiated feedback and allow them to assess their progress and create individualized goals for the next Collaborative Reader Workshop.

By giving students the space to assess their own growth (or lack thereof), you help build more authentic learning—learning that relies on students' personal goals, not only the goals you have determined for the course. This means you can have conversations with them about specific areas of their learning instead of directing them toward what they're doing "wrong."

RACIAL AND CULTURAL RESPONSIVENESS

To be effective, especially in diverse schools, educators must continually ask themselves how their racial and cultural identity impacts what happens in the classroom: the teaching materials they select, the lessons and assessments they plan, and their interactions with students. This is especially important since, according to the U.S. Department of Education (2012), more than 80 percent of schoolteachers are white even as the public school population grows more racially diverse.

When Jason Reynolds, author of popular young adult novels like *All American Boys* and *A Long Way Down*, was asked how he got into writing, he made it clear that it was *not* because of English class: "The teacher was like, 'Read this book about this man chasing a whale,' and I'm like, *bruh*. . . . Nothing that's happening in these books is happening in my neighborhood" (Krug 2017).

It may be reasonable for an English teacher to argue that *Moby Dick* is a classic piece of literature worth studying to learn about symbolism and human condition, but it didn't work for Reynolds. If Reynolds had had the opportunity to read books of his choice *alongside* the book "about this man chasing a whale," he could have made text-to-self connections, found more joy in reading, and formed reading habits early than age seventeen.

Although effective English teachers make an effort to select diverse texts for whole-class study, Collaborative Reader Workshop is another way to differentiate literacy instruction and take another small step toward racial equity through shared citizenship. Rather than depending on a traditional, hierarchical structure, Collaborative Reader Workshop is inclusive, allowing all students the opportunity to see themselves in the literature they study, even if they can't always see themselves in the whole-class novels. The National Council of Teachers of English (NCTE) confirmed this in their 2019 "Statement on Independent Reading": "This practice can also affirm students' own experiences of a world they potentially feel very isolated in."

Representation matters. It validates that individual students' stories—and any perspectives different from the stories they see in canonical English texts—exist and are worthy of thinking and writing about in English class.

Robin DiAngelo, author of *What Does It Mean to Be White?* (2016), points out that most Americans avoid talking about race outside of their own racial groups, which "limits our intellectual, psychic, and emotional growth" and "prevents us from building and sustaining authentic relationships across

---

TEACHER TIP: MIRRORS AND WINDOWS

Raquel McGee, an English teacher at Oak Park and River Forest High School, a diverse Chicagoland public high school, recommends thinking about equity through the metaphor of mirrors and windows—an approach to equity that originates with Rudine Sims-Bishop (1990) and was popularized by organizations like Teaching Tolerance and the Black Caucus of the National Council of Teachers of English (NCTE).

"A balanced reading diet requires students to read within their world (mirrors) and outside their worlds (windows)," McGee explains. "Collaborative Reader Workshop offers a practical, systematic way to achieve this goal."

Although self-selected, independent reading allows students to read diverse perspectives and grow empathy without explicit instruction in equity, you may choose to use discussion day to help your students think deliberately about the mirrors and windows in their chosen texts. This could be a one-pager prompt or a discussion day focus.

racial lines" (18). Collaborative Reader Workshop is a rare opportunity both for students to bring diverse racial and cultural perspectives into conversation and, furthermore, to practice this kind of discussion, one that doesn't shy away from difference.

Students who are more comfortable talking about diversity can model this practice for students who are less comfortable or feel that the topic is taboo. Since these students may never think about picking up a book about someone who looks or lives differently than they do, these discussions are a chance to experience diversity in a way they otherwise wouldn't.

Although social status and language don't automatically determine academic achievement, it's been documented again and again that students who have background experiences that differ from those valued by mainstream society often face a more difficult road to success in the education environment. Collaborative Reader Workshop discussion days are a way to build a community of literacy that includes everyone in the room, regardless of identity. When everyone is writing and sharing about a different text that they chose on their own, students know that you trust them to introduce and discuss material. They know that their interests and values matter.

And face it: some of your students interact with administration only when they're in trouble. To those students, it feels like their dean is just a disciplinarian, someone they deal with when their teachers don't want to deal with them anymore. So when their dean comes into their English class, sits in a circle, and talks about books they love, suddenly those students see the dean not only as a reader but also as someone interested in talking to them about something other than their detentions. In Collaborative Reader Workshop, all students, including those who interact with adults positively, negatively, or not at all, have this opportunity to engage with adults in a neutral context, just chatting about books.

During Collaborative Reader Workshop discussions, administrators, coaches, and teachers support literacy learning in ways not commonly experienced at the high school level. The discussions simulate a "public sphere," Jürgen Habermas's concept of a neutral social space for individuals to voice opinions, regardless of social status (Grbesa 2003, 110). It doesn't matter that the students are younger than their facilitators or coming from different backgrounds; in the space of Collaborative Reader Workshop, they can be experts whose knowledge and interests are valued.

It isn't possible to create a true public sphere in a classroom since teachers and administrators inherently hold power over the students, but Collaborative Reader Workshop is a way to create more neutrality in your classrooms, giving power to student voices. The classroom becomes a space where both students and adults have the opportunity to make choices and to communicate, for a while at least, on relatively equal footing. Students enjoy these discussion days when their opinions and thoughts about their books are valued as highly as the adult sitting next to them.

GENDER RESPONSIVENESS: A NOTE ABOUT BOYS

Much has been made about how male students experience school differently than female students. Although reading proficiency rates are dismal for both genders, the gap between males and females has been widening "with female students outperforming male students in all three reading contexts—literary reading, reading for information, and reading to perform a task" (NEA 2007, 13).

The good news is that choice works for everyone. Atwell (2007) states that interest drives achievement regardless of "testosterone or neuron density" (96). When all readers get to choose their own reading materials, boys can find topics that hold their interest, leading them to practice with the same frequency as the female students.

In their analysis of their male students' literacy habits, Michael Smith and Jeffrey Wilhelm (2002) emphasize the importance of making literacy more social (198). They found that boys embraced literacy that stemmed from relationships. Although a male student may feel that it's not socially acceptable for him to be a reader, he may find that it does feel okay to read and love a book his dad recommended to him. Acknowledging the significance of relationships means finding ways to create class structures, like Collaborative Reader Workshop discussions, that emphasize sharing.

STUDENT STORY: ALEC BREAKS THE HATE

Alec was a charismatic, friendly, and funny football player who repeatedly stated how much he "hated reading." *Every day.* For some students, this is meant as a challenge. Not Alec. He earnestly hated reading and was convinced there was no book that could make him like it. *Ever.*

Then he broke up with his girlfriend, and a student who almost always had a goofy grin on his face was frowning and laying his head on his desk. The next week he suffered an injury while playing football and came to school in a leg brace and crutches, unable to play for months.

Of course, he still hated reading. Books wouldn't help him. Nothing would.

Then Mrs. Fleck gave him Robyn Schneider's *The Beginning of Everything*, a young adult novel about a star tennis player coping with an injury that ended his tennis career. It just so happened that this injury was from a car accident that happened after he caught his girlfriend cheating on him at a party. Mrs. Fleck told Alec both of these things in a whispered—and very personalized—book talk during ten minutes of reading. He wasn't excited about it, but with some gentle nudging, he said he'd "give it a try."

He finished it within a week.

He and Mrs. Fleck talked about it every single day, and he even emailed her in all caps after he read a part toward the end (which we won't spoil for you). Alec realized that with the right story at the right time, reading *could* be something worth doing.

CLOSING THOUGHTS

Throughout history, literacy education "has always required permission, sanction, assistance, coercion" (Brandt 2010, 16). Students read because they have to. They read because there will be a test. They are coerced—for better or worse—into learning the types of literacy valued by their teachers, schools, districts, and society. And as all former students know, sometimes students are simply less enthusiastic about the content they are told they *have* to learn. It's not an uncommon experience to reread a novel you thought you hated when your teacher assigned it only to find that it's actually enjoyable—when no one is making you read it.

Collaborative Reader Workshop sidesteps the goals of the larger school environment and allows students from diverse backgrounds and with diverse abilities to engage in and share what interests them. Maybe your school community would not allow you to use *The Hate U Give* by Angie Thomas—a story about what happens to a black high school student after her friend is the victim of an unjust police shooting—as a whole-class text, but in Collaborative Reader Workshop, students may choose to read and write about *The Hate U Give* and discuss its complicated themes with adults they trust. And they begin to trust that their perspectives matter.

The next chapter explores the importance of building a community of literacy in your classroom—and building.

START PLANNING!

1. How does your racial or cultural background show up in your pedagogy?
2. How do you currently differentiate for diverse learners? What's working? What could be better?
3. Which voices and experiences are currently represented in your curriculum?

Chapter Ten

Why It Works

Lifelong Reading Habits

> The opportunity for students in your workshops to hear what other students are reading and to see their growing interest in books—to witness that others in the class are experiencing the same things as them—well, that's transformative. It always started with this lovely mix of kids who were readers and kids who have faked reading for years. But by the end, there would be this class of readers. And those students' lives will forever be impacted by what you offered them: Time. Interest. And books.—Janet Anderson, high school librarian

The previous three chapters detailed all the good that comes from Collaborative Reader Workshop: improved test scores, healthier social-emotional lives, and differentiated learning for individual students. All of this leads to the primary reason many teachers love Collaborative Reader Workshop: we want our students to be lifelong readers. We want our students to practice the habits practiced by adult readers. We want them to be empathetic, active participants in the adult world.

This is a refrain throughout the most important texts on teaching literacy. Kelly Gallagher (2009) reminds teachers to "never lose sight" of this priority: "What our students read in school is important; what they read the rest of their lives is more important" (117). In *Readicide,* Gallagher explains that his students are always reading two books at a time: one self-selected for pleasure and one for the class.

Penny Kittle (2013) agrees that this equilibrium between self-selected and whole-class reading is key: "If we want to create lifelong, satisfied readers, we need a balance between the careful study of complex texts and time to pursue personal passions in books of choice for pure pleasure. The key is we have to *teach* both" (34). In *180 Days* (2018), Gallagher and Kittle advocate for a 50–25–25 balance: 50 percent self-selected, 25 percent limited choice as in book clubs, and 25 percent as whole-class texts (46). After all, this is how many adults read: you have articles and journals that you're reading for work, and then before bed, you pick up the novel from the bedside table.

Help your students discover that there's something satisfying in both: it can feel fulfilling to pick through the puzzle of a complicated text, to understand it, and—yes—to earn A's on the work. And it's fulfilling in a different way to get lost in a self-selected novel, to get into "the zone," as Nancie Atwell calls it, so that you have to blink and reorient yourself to the world when it's time to put down the book.

This chapter details how and why Collaborative Reader Workshop transforms our student readers into lifelong readers by fostering growth mindset, establishing reading habits, and orienting our students into a community of readers.

CREATING GROWTH MINDSET

As examined in chapter 7, most students don't read outside of school, so giving them time to read books they enjoy during English class is the only chance they have to develop the habits of lifelong readers. For a lot of students, though, that means you're asking them to do something they haven't done since they were little kids.

How many times have students told you that they just don't like reading? They have already determined before entering our classrooms that they are not readers. Most of the time, they're convinced that this class, like all their previous English classes, won't make a difference. So part of the job of making lifelong readers also means convincing students that they can grow into what they think they're not.

Growth mindset is the belief that learners can get smarter. If students have a growth mindset, they believe they can improve, which means they put in more effort and, consequently, see more growth. But when students believe they cannot achieve—that someone either is or is not a reader—they don't put in the effort to grow and, therefore, don't see growth.

Some say it's a self-fulfilling cycle: they think it's the kids' bad attitudes. The kids who call themselves nonreaders don't even try, so of course they fall further behind.

But Collaborative Reader Workshop agrees with Kittle: we have to ask ourselves whether these students are reading texts that are not helping them (2013, 12). If the text is too hard, they can't read fluidly. If they can't see any part of themselves or their lives in the text, they don't have a purpose for reading and are easily distracted. In both cases, they wonder what the point is. Often, they stop reading.

Fortunately, science has discovered the neuroplasticity of the brain. We know that the brain rewires itself in response to learning. When networks in the brain are not being used, the brain does some "neuronal pruning" to rid itself of what's not needed. This is why, as educator Jeffrey Wilhelm (2010) puts it, "assigning and assessing are not enough to get the job done" (38). Rather, teachers—especially teachers of students who do not primarily speak standard English—need to avoid traditional teacher-led pedagogy and try new, complex, student-led tasks to allow for the rewiring of students' brains.

Collaborative Reader Workshop is the type of innovative literacy practice that helps students learn to see themselves as readers. When you give students choice and time to read what they want to read, they read. Suddenly the kid who hasn't read a book since middle school has finished three novels or is halfway through a long Stephen King book. Students hear about new books each week and begin to understand their reading preferences. They plan to read that book their friend told them about during last week's workshop discussion. And when they start to identify as readers, they have more confidence and interest in doing literacy work.

CULTIVATING LONG-LASTING READING HABITS

So how do you inspire students to have a growth mindset? Consider what students learn about literacy in the traditional English class: literature is a puzzle with a hidden message that the teacher knows and that you need to guess. You need to figure out what it is on your own because talking to another student is cheating.

Collaborative Reader Workshop pushes students to start doing what adult readers do: come up with their own reasons for reading, discover their own ideas about what's meaningful in the text, and talk about it with other readers. This is why adults join book clubs: it's enjoyable to read a book, but it's even more enjoyable—and intellectually stimulating—to discuss and debate that book afterward.

In its *Framework for Success in Postsecondary Writing*, the National Council of Teachers of English (NCTE) endorses eight habits of mind, or ways of approaching learning, that are essential for students to be successful after high school graduation. Although NCTE, working alongside the National Writing Project and the Council of Writing Program Administrators, is primarily concerned with college writing in this report, its work indicates that these habits of mind foster success in a variety of disciplines.

> **TEACHER TIP: REMEMBER WHAT YOU LEARNED IN YOUR BOOK CLUB**
>
> Last year, my book club read *The Sense of an Ending* by Julian Barnes. Going in, I knew it was an award-winning book but knew nothing about the plot. When I finished, I thought it was entertaining and beautifully written but didn't quite understand the ending. I was kind of let down.
>
> Then I went to book club.
>
> It wasn't until I discussed *Sense of an Ending* with my fellow book club members that my understanding of the book started evolving. As we debated the ending (Wait! Who's Adrian's father?) and they pointed to moments that slipped my notice, I started to see the brilliance—and playfulness—of the novel.
>
> By the end of the discussion, I ranked that novel among my favorites of the year. And isn't that exactly how it goes? It's the discussion, whether it's about a novel, a movie, or a show, that helps you to organize your thoughts, make new realizations, and solidify your feelings.
>
> Self-selected, independent reading has value on its own, but it's discussion—especially with a more adept reader to push your questioning and challenge your opinions—that gives the literacy experience more significance. Sharing your love of a book makes you love it even more.

These are the ways that adults think, so it's important that we provide opportunities for our students to practice these ways of thinking. Table 10.1 defines each habit of mind and shows how Collaborative Reader Workshop allows students to practice it. Chapter 7 covered how reading widely makes you smarter; however, reading widely also helps you form these habits of mind.

Table 10.1. Habits of Mind from the Framework for Success in Postsecondary Writing

Habit of Mind	Definition	How Students Practice the Habit
Curiosity	The desire to know more about the world	Students select reading that aligns with their interests and learn about new books through book talks and Collaborative Reader Workshop discussions.
Openness	The willingness to consider new ways of being and thinking in the world	Students experience other ways of being and thinking through wide reading and during Collaborative Reader Workshop discussions.
Engagement	A sense of investment and involvement in learning	Collaborative Reader Workshop fosters engagement through student choice and relationship building during Collaborative Reader Workshop discussions.

Table 10.1. *Continued*

Habit of Mind	Definition	How Students Practice the Habit
Creativity	The ability to use novel approaches for generating, investigating, and representing ideas	Students have a choice of twenty different one-page prompts to demonstrate reading and writing comprehension, including multiple creative selections.
Persistence	The ability to sustain interest in and attention to short- and long-term projects	Students are expected to meet daily, weekly, and semester-long literacy goals.
Responsibility	The ability to take ownership of one's actions and understand the consequences of those actions for oneself and others	Students learn to recognize their own role in their learning and understand that learning is a shared endeavor.
Flexibility	The ability to adapt to situations, expectations, or demands	Students express their ideas in diverse formats, including one pagers, quick writes, and Collaborative Reader Workshop discussions. Students adapt to changes in groupings as needed.
Metacognition	The ability to reflect on one's own thinking as well as on the individual and cultural processes used to structure knowledge	Students set and reflect on literacy goals each month and use feedback from a one pager or discussion to make improvements on subsequent work.

STUDENT STORY: KHALIL PRACTICES ENGAGEMENT

Consider Khalil, who hated reading when he came into junior English and "hadn't read a book [he] liked ever." What he meant was that he hadn't read a book that he could connect to in a real way.

Khalil was an incredibly talented basketball player, so starting him off with *Hooper* by Geoff Herbach tapped into this passion. He got into the story because of basketball, but he connected with the character's inner conflicts and struggles that go beyond basketball, too. He went on to read *Every Day* by David Levithan, *How It Went Down* by Kekla Magoon, and *Be More Chill* by Ned Vizzini—all very different stories with varied characters, perspectives, and engaging storylines.

Not only did he become a habitual reader (when he was given time and space to read), but he also became a leader in the classroom as he encouraged others to read the books he had just finished. They knew him for his laid-back demeanor and athletic skills, but now they trusted him as an authentic peer reader—if Khalil liked it, it *had* to be good.

And Khalil, in his end-of-year reflection, poignantly stated, "I still don't love books, unless they're the good ones. But I like having all these books to tell people to read. It gives me something to talk about other than just basketball."

TEACHER TIP: READ WHAT THEY READ

Rob Baker, an English teacher at Barrington High School, tried reading manga for the first time because of a student in his discussion group. He originally didn't think he'd enjoy *Orange* by Ichigo Takano when a student suggested it to him. But when he gave it a try, he enjoyed both the story and the manga illustrations.

"I frequently advise students to read in all genres, to not limit themselves to just one or two," Rob said when reflecting on his reading habits. "If you finish a book and suddenly don't feel any enthusiasm to start another one, maybe it's because you need to shake it up a bit and read something different than you normally do. Personally, I'll read anything—YA, mystery, sci-fi, biography/memoir, sports, history, horror, science, current events, kids' books, whatever—and I find that constantly switching it up keeps me enthusiastic as a reader and able to talk with more students about whatever interests them."

Adult readers have room to grow, too, and as the facilitators reflect on their growth on discussion days, they model these habits of mind, showing curiosity about other readers' ideas, openness when someone says something they disagree with, engagement in the tasks of the discussion, and metacognition about their reading habits and goals.

Reading in a traditional class structure—without choice and without collaborative discussion that fosters an exchange of recommendations—loses this meaning. Students in Collaborative Reader Workshop become curious about other books and experiences and learn to be open about stories they wouldn't have considered before. They practice metacognition when they set and work toward their own goals and persistence as they return to the discussion group again with new goals to meet and new books to discuss. In short, Collaborative Reader Workshop models how adults live literate lives and provides a structure for students to practice these ways of thinking.

Perhaps it's because of these habits of mind that adults who read generally acquire higher achieving jobs and report more opportunities for career growth (NEA 2007). They also volunteer and vote at higher rates than adults who don't read. Reading correlates with living a civically engaged life.

BUILDING READER COMMUNITIES

Adult readers want to be part of a community; they join book clubs, post on the social media site Goodreads, read book reviews, and listen to podcasts about books. And even though students participate in communities on teams, in clubs, and on social media, they tend to see learning as an individual endeavor, something they do quietly in a classroom or alone in a library.

Yet in its 2018 "Call to Action," NCTE found that "discussion-based approaches to academic literacy content are strongly linked to student achievement." They quote findings by educator Jeffrey Wilhelm:

- Learning is social and transactional.
- Learning is an apprenticeship into a community of practice.
- Learners move on a continuum from novice to expert.

This is why it's not enough to give students time to read independently (though that's a great start). Collaborative Reader Workshop is social: students discuss their ideas with other readers. It's transactional: adult facilitators model effective thinking while exchanging ideas with student readers. It's an apprenticeship that helps move learners from novice to expert as they discuss how, why, and what they read. When students know they have an authentic audience for their ideas, they think more deeply; when they engage adult readers in conversation, they mimic and practice expert ways of thinking and talking about literature; and when they have time and space to process their thoughts aloud, they get more practice with reading comprehension.

Although some educators give students reading time while they grade or sit at their desk doing other work, our structure requires the teacher to be an active participant as well. If you want your students to consider your book recommendations, you need to follow up on their recommendations, too.

For example, when you reveal to your discussion group that you're reading—and *loving*—a book one of them suggested, this transactional moment solidifies a relationship between you and your student while also encouraging that student to be an active member of the reader community. For students who struggle to fit into other communities, this connection with a trusted adult gives them a reason to keep coming to English and makes it easier for them to speak up. It's less frightening now that their teacher shared first. Without this collaborative structure, a student's ideas may have remained only partially developed in her mind or on paper.

Since literacy is a community practice—what educational psychologist Lauren Resnik (1990) defines as "a set of cultural practices that people engage in"—literacy teachers must provide opportunities for students to be apprentices, training in the literacy practices of the world outside of academics (170). Resnick (1990) identifies three types of literary practice: useful literacy, informational literacy, and pleasurable literacy with the defining feature being that a reader "picks up and puts down a book or a story at will" (182).

English teachers want their students to find pleasure in reading, yet in the traditional English classroom, students are required to read texts chosen by the instructor, meet due dates set by the instructor, and answer questions to prove to the instructor that they have read. Though these activities help to hold students accountable, they also imply that reading is something teachers need to force them to do; it's not a pleasure in its own right. Although Collaborative Reader Workshop requires students to write one-pager responses, it is the apprenticeship—the book talks and discussions with other readers—that gives students training in adult reading habits.

So what do adult readers do? You pick up books you're interested in and put them down when you lose interest. You skim if something seems less important or redundant, and you slow down and reread if you realize you are struggling to grasp the author's point. You annotate, in your own style, marking lines you love or want to remember or have questions about. And of course, you share what you read with your friends, family, and whoever else will listen. You want your students to see these habits "live" in your classroom and adopt them as they leave your school and venture out into the world.

CLOSING THOUGHTS

There was once a debate in the United States about whether citizens—both adults and adolescents—actually were reading less than they did in prior decades. We know now, beyond a doubt, that this is the case.

And yet, just when successful educators have suggested how to fix this problem, the debate has shifted. Now we're wondering whether it's a problem after all. Does it matter if we prefer Instagram to novels? If most of our reading happens on Twitter or Buzzfeed listicles? If nearly half of all Americans don't read books? Is it actually a problem or is it just *different*?

Here's what the National Endowment for the Arts (2007) says: reading is "both fundamental and irreplaceable for democracy" (6). If reading helps our kids to become more active and successful adults, then we can't pretend that the types of reading they do on their phones is enough. We can't control what our students do outside of the classroom, so we have to make the classroom into a place where reading happens. That means students need this. They need access to books they're curious about, time and space to read those books, and a community of other readers to discuss them with.

START PLANNING!

1. How can you help students build effective reading habits?
2. How can you foster authentic connection to fellow readers inside and outside of your classroom?
3. How can you model lifelong reading habits in your classroom?

Epilogue

Do you teach English?

Or do you teach students?

Collaborative Reader Workshop began when we stopped trying to race the calendar to squeeze in a certain number of books by the end of the school year and started to brainstorm new ways our students could develop literacy skills, when we stopped to take a breath and thought about our students as individual humans with individual needs that couldn't be summed up with a test score.

A few years ago, we started feeling that pressure that comes along in May. We're sure you've felt it, too. We were running out of time. We wouldn't be able to fit in a whole new novel.

Half-jokingly, Stephanie made a suggestion: "Hey, why don't we just let them read what they want for the last three weeks?"

Jolene contemplated this for a moment. "I guess we could pair it with the personal narrative writing we wanted to do."

"Yes!"

"And give them practice with conflict, structure, characterization—you know, all the narrative writing stuff."

"Yes!"

"So how do we structure it?" Jolene wondered.

"I mean, this is all in my head, but hear me out. We could have kids talk in small groups at the end of each week about whatever book they're already reading. Like a book club maybe?"

"Keep talking...."

And we did. The pilot group of Collaborative Reader Workshop was made up of average-level juniors. Not many of these students thought of themselves as readers or bought in to class activities. Yet, each Friday at the end of that year when their dean or coach or history teacher walked into the room, there was a buzz of excitement in the air. It was weird to see the new faces. But it was also kind of exciting.

In their end-of-year reflections, so many of our students said they hadn't seen the point of independent reading—until those last few weeks. They kind of liked those last few weeks.

Knowing all we know about the importance of reading and how it helps students become smarter, more capable people, couldn't we just *tell* them how important it is and encourage them to read outside of class? Couldn't we just photocopy the National Endowment for the Art's 2007 report and pass it out to parents on back-to-school night?

If your students are anything like ours, that won't do the trick. They're busy people. They have club meetings and sports practice and homework. They have Snapchat and YouTube. If we assign reading outside of school, some of them might meet the requirement to earn the grade and others might find ways to fake it.

But the path to literacy can be paved only with consistent reading. And the research is there: most teenagers aren't going to make time to read on their own. So, knowing that, it's our job to give them that time.

We hope that this book helps you adapt Collaborative Reader Workshop to fit your classroom needs. We hope it helps you find a way to fit independent reading alongside your department's curricular goals and create a reading schedule that works for your calendar.

But we also hope you see that Collaborative Reader Workshop goes beyond academic standards to that core need of every human being: connection with others. Although Collaborative Reader workshop offers time and space to practice all the important literacy skills demanded of our students, to us it's more important that it helps them become well-rounded and thoughtful people, that it makes them feel part of a community. We want them to remember how their dean made them laugh talking about *Carter Finally Gets It* by Brent Crawford. We want them to remember how they immediately added *The Happiness Project* by Gretchen Rubin to their Goodreads list after the school psychologist told them about it.

Most importantly, we want to keep getting emails like the one we recently received from Maddy in her first year of college. She asked us for book recommendations because she wanted to try to read in her dorm room for ten minutes a night before she went to bed. She told us some of her friends were planning to try it, too.

This is how we positively impact each other and grow as readers, learners, and people: by building a community. Once you galvanize students' interest in reading, the landscape of teaching looks radically differently. They *want* to read. They do it without you asking them to. They no longer see it as work. For English teachers, there should be no higher priority.

So if you take one thing from this book, let it be that priority. And moving forward, we hope that you and your students read like it matters (because it does), write about your reading worlds (because the reading world connects to the real world), and talk to each other as humans beings (because that's what English class is all about).

Thank you for reading,
Stephanie and Jolene

Appendix
Book Lists

We can't list *every* book our students have enjoyed because there are too many! But the lists in this appendix offer a place to start for those of you who are unfamiliar with young adult or popular literature or those of you who need a recommendation for specific student. Sites like Goodreads and What Should I Read Next? are other tools to help expand your knowledge of books students will love.

Have fun! And good luck!

ARE YOU AFRAID OF THE DARK?

If your students enjoy horror movies or tell you with a shy smile that they like stories that are "dark" or "messed-up stuff," try

- *Room* by Emma Donoghue
- *Gone Girl* or *Dark Places* by Gillian Flynn
- *Horns* by Joe Hill
- *The Grip of It* by Jac Jemc
- *It*, *Misery*, or *The Shining* by Stephen King
- *Darkly Dreaming Dexter* by Jeff Lindsay
- *I Hunt Killers* by Barry Lyga
- *Rot & Ruin* by Jonathan Maberry
- *Arrowood* by Laura McHugh
- *The Lovely Bones* by Alice Sebold

FEATURED BOOK: *I HUNT KILLERS* BY BARRY LYGA

Jazz's dad is famous. For serial murders. Sixteen-year-old Jazz was raised by a serial killer father who taught him the ways of his profession. But Jazz doesn't want to be anything like his dad, who is currently in prison. The problem is that no one in his town believes him. Suddenly copycat murders break out, and Jazz is on a mission to find out who this new killer is so that everyone knows it's not *him*.

How to sell it: If students love the show *Dexter*, this is like reading about a teenage version of the character. If they haven't seen the show, mention that some of the chapters are from the victims' perspectives and others can give gruesome descriptions of crime scenes—you can even tell them they might not even be able to handle it (because when you tell a teenager not to do something . . .).

FAMILY LOVE AND LOSS

Losing yourself in someone else's story can be an effective way to process grief. When you read that someone else has experienced loss, it can make you feel less isolated. These books are useful for that. They're also useful for someone who just wants a good cry. If you have a student who is interested in stories that deal with hard family stuff, grief, and/or loss, try

- *Far from the Tree* by Robin Benway
- *Saint Anything* by Sarah Dessen
- *The Virgin Suicides* by Jeffrey Eugenides
- *If I Stay* and *Where She Went* by Gayle Forman
- *All the Bright Places* by Jennifer Niven
- *Before I Fall* by Lauren Oliver
- *A List of Cages* by Robin Roe
- *I Am Not Your Perfect Mexican Daughter* by Erika Sanchez
- *The Lovely Bones* by Alice Sebold
- *They Both Die at the End* by Adam Silvera
- *The Art of Racing in the Rain* by Garth Stein
- *Belzhar* by Meg Wolitzer

FEATURED BOOK: *BELZHAR* BY MEG WOLITZER

Jam suffers a terrible tragedy when her boyfriend dies. She's so depressed that she can't function. Her parents don't know what to do to help her. They decide to send her to the Wooden Bar, a boarding school for "emotionally fragile youth," with a bunch of other kids who don't want to be there. Classic setup. Plus, it has a cool English class.

How to sell it: Read the scene where their English teacher introduces herself and Griffin Foley says the teacher "made a big mistake with me." Then read the end of that scene where their teacher challenges each one to tell their own story, even though this is extremely hard to do. Let your students know that's your hope for them, too.

GENRE BENDERS

Books that play with genre and text structure can be stepping-stones into reading for hesitant readers. For students who love to read, it can be fun when authors play with how they tell stories or with how the text looks on the page. If your students want to read poetry, novels in verse, or other experimental styles, try

- *The Poet X* by Elizabeth Acevedo
- *2fish* by Jhené Aiko
- *The Crossover* by Kwame Alexander
- *The Perks of Being a Wallflower* by Stephen Chbosky
- *I Hate Everyone but You* by Gaby Dunn and Allison Raskin
- *The Shark and the Goldfish* by Jon Gordon
- *Illuminae* by Amie Kaufman
- *Milk and Honey* by Rupi Kaur
- *The Princess Saves Herself in This One* by Amanda Lovelace
- *Monster* by Walter Dean Myers
- *Long Way Down* by Jason Reynolds
- *I Wrote This for You* by Iain S. Thomas

FEATURED BOOK: *2FISH* BY JHENÉ AIKO

Songwriter and poet Jhené Aiko shares her poetry in this compact collection that includes journal entries from when she was in high school (and photocopies of the actual pages of her journal). Her work talks about heartbreak, loss, grief, and identity, to name a few. It's a quick and engaging read.

How to sell it: Show the photocopied pages from her journal and talk about how they show her process—where she crossed lines out and how she added words in the margins. Then have students think about their own writing process and how it may look different in their personal writing than it does at school.

GET YOUR THRILLS

Some students are interested in mystery or suspense but don't necessarily want to be scared. For these students, try

- *The Leaving* by Tara Altebrando
- *Stolen* by Lucy Christopher
- *Push Play* by Eric Devine
- *The Woman in the Window* by A. J. Finn
- *The Unfinished Life of Addison Stone* by Adele Griffin
- *The Girl on the Train* by Paula Hawkins
- *The Good Girl* by Mary Kubica
- *One of Us Is Lying* by Karen McManus
- *Panic* by Lauren Oliver
- *Behind Closed Doors* by B. A. Paris
- *Hunt for the Bamboo Rat* by Graham Salisbury
- *Belzhar* by Meg Wolitzer

FEATURED BOOK: *PANIC* BY LAUREN OLIVER

Panic is an underground game run by the young people in a small, dead-end town. Throughout your senior year, you chip in to the pot of money, and on the night of graduation, any senior can officially enter the competition—by jumping off a cliff.

The challenges get more intense—and more dangerous—from there. The cops want to shut it down, but the seniors are secretive about how the tasks are communicated. Teens have died playing this game, but the last competitor standing wins enough money to escape the small town in search for a better life. That poses the question: is it worth it?

How to sell it: Tell the students it's a lot like the movie *Nerve*. If they like that story, they'll love this one. Then read the opening chapter from Heather's perspective when she jumps off the cliff and into the game.

LOLS AND SPORTS

If your students say they hate reading, but you know that they enjoy sports, like to laugh, or are easily distracted, try

- *Me and Earl and the Dying Girl* by Jesse Andrews
- *Ready Player One* by Ernest Cline
- *Carter Finally Gets It* by Brent Crawford
- *Hooper* by Geoff Herbach
- *Boy21* by Matthew Quick
- *The Beginning of Everything* by Robyn Schneider
- *Winger* by Andrew Smith
- *The Spectacular Now* by Tim Tharp
- *Be More Chill* by Ned Vizzini

FEATURED BOOK: *WINGER* BY ANDREW SMITH

Ryan Dean West got in trouble at his boarding school for hacking into a teacher's cell phone to call his best friend. Now, he's stuck in "Opportunity Hall" with the kids who cause the most trouble in the school. He's a winger on the school's rugby team, an endlessly funny and self-deprecating storyteller, and an amateur cartoonist (drawings are included in the book).

There is a lot of swearing, authentic teenage "dude voice," and LGBTQ elements. It looks big, but every student who has ever whined about how long it is ends up loving it.

How to sell it: Just read aloud the first page—but consider your audience! There's a lot of questionable language.

LOVE YOU LIKE A LOVE SONG

There's nothing like a good love story, right? If your students want to read about relationships, try

- *Emmy & Oliver* by Robin Benway
- *The Selection* by Kiera Cass
- *Fault Line* by C. Desir
- *Someone Like You* by Sarah Dessen
- *To All the Boys I've Loved Before* by Jenny Han
- *Why We Broke Up* by Daniel Handler
- *Every Day* by David Levithan
- *I'll Give You the Sun* by Jandy Nelson
- *Anna and the French Kiss* by Stephanie Perkins
- *Carry On, Eleanor & Park*, or *Fangirl* by Rainbow Rowell
- *Aristotle and Dante Discover the Secrets of the Universe* by Benjamin Alire Sáenz
- *Everything, Everything* or *The Sun Is Also a Star* by Nicola Yoon

---

FEATURED BOOK: *EMMY & OLIVER* BY ROBIN BENWAY

When Emmy and Oliver were seven years old, Oliver's dad was supposed to bring him back after a long weekend.

But Oliver never came back.

Ten years later, the police find Oliver and bring him home—but can Emmy and Oliver rekindle their BFF status all these years later?

How to sell it: Talk about the fact that, after all this time, Oliver's got mixed feelings about being "home." Although his father kidnapped Oliver, he was still Oliver's dad. And it was only life Oliver knew. Hint at the love connection. And read them some of the incredibly realistic and fast-paced dialogue.

PICTURES—NOT JUST FOR KIDS

Illustrations are another awesome way to get hesitant readers to pick up a book. There's nothing wrong with superhero comic books, but for Collaborative Reader Workshop, push your comic book lovers to try an extended graphic novel or a traditional prose novel that's interspersed with illustrations. For stories with visual art, try

- *The Absolutely True Diary of a Part-Time Indian* by Sherman Alexie
- *My Friend Dahmer* by Derf Backderf
- *Kindred: A Graphic Novel Adaptation* by Octavia Butler, adapted by Damian Duffy, illustrated by John Jennings
- *Through the Woods* by Emily Carroll
- *Why We Broke Up* by Daniel Handler, illustrated by Maira Kalman
- *The Kite Runner: Graphic Novel* by Khaled Hosseini, illustrated by Fabio Celoni and Mirka Andolfo
- *Watchmen* by Alan Moore, illustrated by Dave Gibbons
- *Yummy: The Last Days of a Southside Shorty* by G. Neri, illustrated by Randy DuBurke
- *A Monster Calls* by Patrick Ness, from the ideas of Siobhan Dowd, illustrated by Jim Kay
- *Persepolis* by Marjane Satrapi
- *Winger* by Andrew Smith
- *Sisters* by Raina Telgemeier
- *Blankets* by Craig Thompson
- *American Born Chinese* by Gene Yang

FEATURED BOOK: *THROUGH THE WOODS* BY EMILY CARROLL

This graphic novel collection is made up of some of the most terrifying stories we've ever read. Depicting terrifying tales like a husband who hides his wife's skeleton, this psychologically thrilling collection is perfect to book-talk around Halloween.

How to sell it: This one sells itself with the spooky images. Talk about the fact that you went in expecting to be able to handle it (it's just some scary drawings, right?) but then had to read it with the lights on—and only while other people were around.

REDEFINING NORMAL

Make a point to normalize LGBTQ+ stories by book-talking them as regularly as you do books with heterosexual or cis protagonists. For LGBTQ+ stories, try

- *Simon vs. the Homo Sapiens Agenda* by Becky Albertalli
- *Some Assembly Required* by Arin Andrews
- *Look Past* by Eric Devine
- *Will Grayson, Will Grayson* by John Green and David Levithan
- *Beyond Magenta* by Susan Kuklin
- *Boy Meets Boy* by David Levithan
- *Every Day* by David Levithan
- *You Know Me Well* by Nina LaCour and David Levithan
- *I'll Give You the Sun* by Jandy Nelson
- *If I Was Your Girl* by Meredith Russo
- *Aristotle and Dante Discover the Secrets of the Universe* by Benjamin Alire Sáenz
- *What If It's Us* by Adam Silvera and Becky Albertalli
- *Afterworlds* by Scott Westerfeld

FEATURED BOOK: *BOY MEETS BOY* BY DAVID LEVITHAN

This story is exactly what it sounds like: a boy meets—and falls for—another boy. But what makes this book special is the lack of trauma. Paul and Noah are at a dream high school where all genders, sexual preferences, and any other ways of living and being are accepted and celebrated.

This is a warm and wonderful love story with a cast of hilarious, thoughtful, and interesting characters that make readers think about the first love that they experienced or that they one day hope to have.

How to sell it: Play an excerpt of the audiobook (you can find free samples of it online) to help the students hear the voices. Talk about the diversity of the high school, and use this as a jumping-off point to ask students to think about what their ideal school would be like.

Appendix

THIS IS REAL LIFE

In our celebrity-obsessed culture, sometimes a famous memoir is just the thing a student needs to get into reading. These stories are often partly hilarious and partly inspirational. If your students are interested in stories about famous people, try

- *Modern Romance* by Aziz Ansari
- *Egghead* by Bo Burnham
- *Bossypants* by Tina Fey
- *Dad Is Fat* by Jim Gaffigan
- *Why Not Me?* or *Is Everyone Hanging Out Without Me?* by Mindy Kaling
- *Scrappy Little Nobody* by Anna Kendrick
- *Born a Crime* by Trevor Noah
- *One More Thing* by B. J. Novak
- *Yes Please* by Amy Poehler
- *The Misadventures of Awkward Black Girl* by Issa Rae
- *You Can't Touch My Hair* by Phoebe Robinson
- *The Girl with the Lower Back Tattoo* by Amy Schumer

FEATURED BOOK: *BOSSYPANTS* BY TINA FEY

Tina Fey tells the story of her life from childhood all the way through to her success on *Saturday Night Live* and *30 Rock*. If students enjoy any of her shows or movies, her book is written exactly the way she talks. It's full of both laugh-out-loud moments and inspirational explorations about how she learned to be a boss in large part from *Saturday Night Live* royalty, Lorne Michaels. If students are interested in any leadership positions, this book has a lot of funny and necessary advice on how to be an effective leader.

How to sell it: Play a clip from the introduction read by Tina Fey and hype up the fact that she starred in and wrote *Mean Girls*, especially if your students don't know her from anything else (hard to believe, but it happens). You can find clips of the audiobook on YouTube.

TOUGH STUFF

We can't stop teenagers from being curious about the world around them (and we shouldn't want to). If your students are interested in stories about characters struggling with real-world issues like drugs, addiction, mental health issues, and the like, try

- *Hate List* by Jennifer Brown
- *Bleed Like Me* by C. Desir
- *House Arrest* by K. A. Holt
- *Crank* by Ellen Hopkins
- *Exit, Pursued by a Bear* by E. K. Johnston
- *When We Collided* by Emery Lord
- *How It Went Down* by Kekla Magoon
- *All the Bright Places* by Jennifer Niven
- *A Child Called It* by Dave Pelzer
- *The Way I Used to Be* by Amber Smith
- *Challenger Deep* by Neal Shusterman
- *It's Kind of a Funny Story* by Ned Vizzini

FEATURED BOOK: *HOUSE ARREST* BY K. A. HOLT

This is a story about Timothy, a middle schooler on house arrest. The courts have ordered him to complete a daily journal during his time on house arrest, monitored closely by his parole officer. He writes that journal in verse that isn't so much poetry as lines of mandated thoughts. You find out why he's on house arrest, the complications of his family and life, and how he interacts with the adults assigned by the court (his probation officer, his therapist, etc.). At times you laugh, at times your cry, and the entire time, you root for him against the odds.

How to sell it: Show students the week 2 entry in which Timothy contemplates why he has to write this journal and calls his probation officer a "tool"—then negates that because he was told the judge wouldn't like it.

Appendix

A TWIST ON A CLASSIC

These books are reimagined classic stories or fairy tales, especially ones that students watched as Disney movies when they were kids. If your students are curious about how contemporary writers rework classic stories, try

- *Great* by Sara Benincasa (Retelling of *The Great Gatsby*)
- *Going Bovine* by Libba Bray (Retelling of *Don Quixote*)
- *Beastly* by Alex Flinn (Retelling of *Beauty and the Beast*)
- *Pride and Prejudice and Zombies* by Seth Grahame-Smith
- *Warm Bodies* by Isaac Marion (Retelling of *Romeo and Juliet*)
- *Cinder* by Marissa Meyer (Retelling of *Cinderella*)
- *Orpheus Girl* by Brynne Rebele-Henry (Retelling of *Orpheus*)
- *Home Fire* by Kamila Shamsie (Retelling of *Antigone*)
- *Second Star* by Alyssa B. Sheinmel (Retelling of *Peter Pan*)
- *The Dark Descent of Elizabeth Frankenstein* by Kiersten White (Retelling of *Frankenstein*)

FEATURED BOOK: *WARM BODIES* BY ISAAC MARION

Romeo and Juliet and zombies. This book was made into a film that students might be familiar with, and it tells the story of R (a zombie) who meets and falls in love with Julie (a human whom he doesn't want to eat). The two worlds collide in a classic tale of star-crossed lovers. With zombies. It's a funny twist on a classic.

How to sell it: Play the balcony scene from the film. Chances are good that your students are familiar with this scene from Shakespeare's play. Tell them that the book is even better than the movie, which is awesome.

WE NEED DIVERSE BOOKS

Although young adult literature (YAL) has become more diverse in recent years, most popular YAL features white protagonists who (maybe) have a friend from another background. For stories that center people of color, try

- *To All the Boys I've Loved Before* by Jenny Han
- *The Kiss Quotient* by Helen Hoang
- *A Very Large Expanse of Sea* by Tahereh Mafi
- *There There* by Tommy Orange
- *Gabi, Girl in Pieces* by Isabel Quintero
- *When I Was the Greatest* or *Long Way Down* by Jason Reynolds
- *Aristotle and Dante Discover the Secrets of the Universe* by Benjamin Alire Sáenz
- *I Am Not Your Perfect Mexican Daughter* by Erika Sanchez
- *Dear Martin* by Nic Stone
- *The Hate U Give* or *On the Come Up* by Angie Thomas
- *The Sun Is Also a Star* by Nicola Yoon
- *American Street* by Ibi Zoboi

FEATURED BOOK: *GABI, GIRL IN PIECES* BY ISABEL QUINTERO

Gabi Hernandez writes about her senior year of high school through hilarious prose that often jumps from English into Spanish. Some of it is silly, some heartbreaking, and some shocking—but all so true. She shares stories about her Mexican American experience, her complicated family structure, and her friends and their lives. It's hilarious, witty, authentic, and fun to read.

How to sell it: Read aloud the first pages where she tells the reader about some advice her mother gave her for how girls should behave. (Hint: It has to do with sex—or lack thereof.)

Works Cited

Atwell, Nancie. 2007. *The Reading Zone: How to Help Kids Become Skilled, Passionate, Habitual, Critical Readers.* New York: Scholastic.

———. 1998. *In the Middle: New Understandings about Writing, Reading, and Learning.* Portsmouth, NH: Boynton/Cook.

Beers, Kylene, and Robert E. Probst. 2012. *Notice and Note: Strategies for Close Reading.* Portsmouth, NH: Heinemann.

Brandt, Deborah. 2010. "Sponsors of Literacy." In *Writing and Community Engagement: A Critical Sourcebook.* New York: Bedford/St. Martin's.

Collaborative for Academic, Social, and Emotional Learning (CASEL). 2019. "Core SEL Competencies." https://casel.org/core-competencies.

Darvin, Jacqueline. 2009. "Lessons from the Literacy Club: Hamlet Meets the Lion King after School." *The Language and Literacy Spectrum* 19.

DePaoli, Jennifer L., Matthew N. Atwell, and John Bridgeland. 2017. *Ready to Lead: A National Principal Survey on How Social and Emotional Learning Can Prepare Children and Transform Schools.* N.p.: Civic Enterprises with Hart Research Associates. https://files.eric.ed.gov/fulltext/ED579088.pdf.

DiAngelo, Robin. 2016. *What Does It Mean to Be White? Developing White Racial Literacy.* Rev. ed. New York: Peter Lang.

Gallagher, Kelly. 2009. *Readicide: How Schools Are Killing Reading and What You Can Do about It.* Portland, ME: Stenhouse.

Gallagher, Kelly, and Penny Kittle. 2018. *180 Days: Two Teachers and the Quest to Engage and Empower Adolescents.* Portsmouth, NH: Heinemann.

Goodlad, John I. 2004. *A Place Called School: Twentieth Anniversary Edition.* New York: McGraw-Hill.

Grbeša, Marijana. 2003. "Why If at All Is the Public Sphere a Useful Concept?" *Politicka misao* 40, no. 5.

Kittle, Penny. 2013. *Book Love: Developing Depth, Stamina, and Passion in Adolescent Readers.* Portsmouth, NH: Heinemann.

Krashen, Stephen. 2004. *The Power of Reading: Insights from the Research*. 2nd ed. Westport: CT: Libraries Unlimited.

Krug, Nora. 2017. "How a Kid Who Didn't Read a Book until He Was 17 Grew up to Become a Literary Star." *Washington Post*.

Lausé, Julie. 2004. "Using Reading Workshop to Inspire Lifelong Readers." *The English Journal* 93, no. 5.

Lent, ReLeah Cossett. 2016. *This Is Disciplinary Literacy: Reading, Writing, Thinking, and Doing . . . Content Area by Content Area*. Thousand Oaks, CA: Corwin.

Miller, Donalyn. 2014. *Reading in the Wild: The Book Whisperer's Keys to Cultivating Lifelong Reading Habits*. San Francisco: Jossey-Bass.

National Council of Teachers of English (NCTE). 2019. "Statement on Independent Reading." Washington, DC: NCTE.

———. 2018a. "Call to Action: What We Know about Adolescent Literacy Instruction." Washington, DC: NCTE.

———. 2018b. "Literacy Assessment: Definitions, Principles, and Practices." Washington, DC: NCTE.

———. 2018c. "The Students' Right to Read." Washington, DC: NCTE.

———. 2017. "Statement on Classroom Libraries." Washington, DC: NCTE.

National Endowment for the Arts (NEA). 2018. "U.S. Trends in Arts Attendance and Literary Reading: 2002–2017." Washington, DC: National Endowment for the Arts.

———. 2007. "To Read or Not to Read: A Question of National Importance." Washington, DC: National Endowment for the Arts.

National Governors Association Center for Best Practices, Council of Chief State School Officers. 2010. *Common Core State Standards*. Washington, DC: National Governors Association Center for Best Practices.

Postman, Neal. 1969. *Teaching as a Subversive Activity*. New York: Delta Publishing.

Renaissance. 2018. "The Magic of 15 Minutes: Reading Practice and Reading Growth." *Renaissance Blog*. www.renaissance.com/2018/01/23/blog-magic-15-minutes-reading-practice-reading-growth.

Resnick, Lauren B. 1990. "Literacy in School and Out." *Daedalus* 119, no. 2.

Sims-Bishop, Rudine. 1990. "Mirrors, Windows, and Sliding Glass Doors." *Perspectives: Choosing and Using Books for the Classroom* 6, no. 3.

Smith, Michael W., and Jeffrey D. Wilhelm. 2002. *Reading Don't Fix No Chevys: Literacy in the Lives of Young Men*. Portsmouth, NH: Heinemann.

U.S. Department of Education. 2012. *Characteristics of Public and Private Elementary and Secondary School Teachers in the United Sates: Results from the 2011–12 Schools and Staffing Survey*. Washington, DC: U.S. Department of Education.

Wilhelm, Jeffrey D. 2010. "Literacy and Neuroplasticity: Transforming Our Perspectives and Ourselves." *Voices from the Middle* 17, no. 4.

Wolk, Steven. 2008. "Joy in School." *Educational Leadership* 66, no. 1.

Zomorodi, Manoush. 2017. *Bored and Brilliant: How Spacing out Can Unlock Your Most Productive and Creative Self*. London: St. Martin's Press.

Index

Page references for figures are italicized.

180 Days, 47, 115–116

Acevedo, Elizabeth, 130
adaptations: for elementary, 73, 84; for middle school, *74*; for postsecondary, 73, *74*
Aiko, Jhené, 130
Albertalli, Becky, 88, 135
Alexander, Kwame, 130
Alexie, Sheman, 52, 134
Altebrando, Tara, 131
Anderson, Janet, 115
Andolfo, Mirka, 134
Andrews, Arin, *16*, 102, 135
Andrews, Jesse, 132
Ansari, Aziz, 136
assessment: formative, 57, 65–68; of reading, 25, *26*; of speaking, *92–93*; of writing, 25–28, 57
attention-deficit/hyperactivity disorder (ADHD), *99,* 109
Atwell, Nancie, 47; *In the Middle*, 67, 100; *Reading Zone*, 65, 85–86, 93, 105, 109, 113, 116
audiobooks, 13, *14, 135, 136*

authenticity, 28, 99, 110; of book talks, 15; of discussion, 38, 45, 54, 55, 89, 91, 103, 105, 121; of reading, 24, 53

Backman, Fredrik, 89
Backderf, Derf, 134
Baker, Rob, *120*
Barnes, Julian, 118
Barnes & Noble, 7, 8
Beers, Kylene, 20, *21*, 86
Benincasa, Sara, 138
Benway, Robin, *16, 17*, 129, 133
book talk, 10–15, 20, *32*, 36, 38, 58, 96, 108, *118*; rules of, 11; structure of, 12, *15*; themes, 13
books, when to abandon, 10, 23, 51, 52, 101
Bored and Brilliant, 51
brain development, 104, 117
brainstorming, 27, 58
Brandt, Deborah, 114
Bray, Libba, 138
Bronte, Charlotte, 48
Brown, Jennifer, 137
budget limitations, *8,* 9, 49

Burnham, Bo, 136
Butler, Octavia, 134

Carroll, Emily, 134
Cass, Kiera, 133
CASEL. *See* Collaborative for Academic, Social, and Emotional Learning
CCSS. *See* Common Core State Standards
Celoni, Fabio, 134
censorship, *13,* 52–53
Chbosky, Stephen, 130
Christopher, Lucy, 131
classroom library, 6–8, 49, 52, *102*
Cline, Ernest, 132
Coates, Ta-Nehisi, 102
Collaborative for Academic, Social, and Emotional Learning (CASEL), 96–104
Collins, Suzanne, 89
Common Core State Standards (CCSS): Reading, *22, 26,* 86–88, 89; Speaking and Listening, 92–93; Writing, *22,* 25–26, 90
community: digital, 16, 44; how to build, 55–56, 78, 104, 105, 120–122; outside the classroom, *13, 14,* 31, 32, *40,* 54–55
conferencing, 6, *27,* 31, 36, 50–51, 66–67, 68–69, *70,* 91, 97
Council of Writing Program Administration, 117
Crawford, Brent, 13, 124, 132
Crichton, Michael, *13*
cultural responsiveness, 48, 101–103, 107–108, 110–112, 114, 139
curriculum, mandated, 5, 46–48, 88

Darvin, Jacqueline, 63
decision-making, responsible, 10, 51, 78, *93, 96, 99,* 100–101, 104, 119
democracy, *64, 93,* 120, 122
DePaoli, Jennifer L., 95
Desir, C., 133, 137
Dessen, Sarah, 129, 133
Devine, Eric, 131, 135
dialogue letters, 67

DiAngelo, Robin, 111–112
Dickens, Charles, 23
differentiation, 24, 46–47, 65, 67, 69, 91, 99, 108–110, 111; how to, 67, 99, 109–110
discussion: agenda, 32, 36, 41; focus, *32,* 33–34, 62, 66, 67, *70, 72,* 89; grouping, 42–43, 55–56, 119
diverse books, 101–103, 107–108, 110–112, 114, 139
Donoghue, Emma, 128
Douglass, Frederick, 33
Dowd, Sioban, 134
DuBurke, Randy, 134
Duffy, Damian, 134
Dunn, Gaby, 130

Egan, Jennifer, 52
Elkeles, Simone, 6, 27
empathy, developing, 101–103, 105, *111*
English language learners (ELL), *42*
environment, for reading, 7, 9–10, 51
equity, 99, 107–114
Eugenides, Jeffrey, 129

facilitator: guide, 37; recruitment 33, 38–41, 54–55, 59, *70,* 78
fake reading, 6, 49–51
Fey, Tina, 136
flexibility, 5, 34, 36, 47–48, *59,* 61, *70,* 74, *119*
Finn, A. J., 131
Fitzgerald, F. Scott, 24, *49*
Fitzpatrick, Huntley, *16*
Flinn, Alex, 138
fluency, 85
Flynn, Gillian, 67, 128
Forman, Gayle, 129
Framework for Success in Postsecondary Writing, 117, *118*
Frank, E. R., 101

Gaffigan, Jim, 136
Gallagher, Kelly: *180 Days,* 115–116, 47, 115–116; *Readicide,* 6, *8,* 20, *21,* 86, 90–91, 115

gender responsiveness, 113
Gibbons, Dave, 134
Gioia, Dana, 84
Gladwell, Malcolm, 21
Goodlad, John, 3, 32, 92
Goodreads, 8, 12, 14, 16, 43–44, 58, 120, 124, 127
Gordon, Jon, 130
Grahame-Smith, Seth, 138
graphic novels, 12, 58, 72, 109, 134
Green, John, *98*, 135
growth mindset, 66, 78, 96, 98, 116–117, 120
Grbeša, Marijana, 112
Griffin, Adele, 131

Habermas, Jurgen, 112
habit formation, 3, 6, 11, 30, *40*, 46, 50–53, 62, 68–69, *70, 77–78*, 84, 97, 106, 111–113, 115–118, *119*, 120, 122
Han, Jenny, *16*, 33, 133, 139
Handler, Daniel, 133, 134
Hawkins, Paula, 131
Hill, Joe, 128
Herbach, Geoff, *119*, 132
Hoang, Helen, 139
Holt, K. A., 137
Hopkins, Ellen, 137
Hosseini, Khaled, 134

In the Middle, 67, 100
initiate-respond-evaluate (IRE), 57, 63, 92
Instagram, 16, 68
instruction: student-centered, 19, 25, 50, 108; teacher-centered, 19, 32, 58, 63, 92, 100, 107, 108, 121

James, E. L., *53*
Jemc, Jac, 128
Johnston, E. K., 137

Kaling, Mindy, 136
Kalman, Maira, 134
Kaufman, Amie, 130

Kaur, Rupi, 130
Kay, Jim, 134
Kendrick, Anna, 136
Kiely, Brendan, 47
King, Stephen, 23, 33, 104, 128
Kinney, Jeff, 52
Kirkorsky, Sarah, 95
Kittle, Penny: *180 Days,* 47, 115–116; *Book Love,* 86, 88, 97, 108
Kolbert, Elizabeth, 72, 101
Krashen, Stephen, 85–86, 90
Krug, Nora, 111
Kubica, Mary, 131
Kuklin, Susan, 135

LaCour, Nina, 135
Lause, Julie, 69, 71
learning styles, multiple, 21
Lee, Harper, 48
Lent, ReLeah, 71–72
Levithan, David, *119*, 133, 135
Lexile, 50, 63, 72, *99*
LGBTQ+, 102, 103, 135
library: classroom, 6–7, *8*, 12, 49, 52, *102*; digital, 7–8
Lindsay, Jeff, 128
literary analysis, 23–24, 33, 35, 46, 77, 62–63, 89, 90–91, 100
Lord, Emery, 137
Lovelace, Amanda, 130
Lyga, Barry, *16*, 128

Maberry, Jonathan, 128
Mafi, Tahereh, 139
Magoon, Kekla, *119*, 137
Marion, Isaac, 138
Maslow's hierarchy of needs, 105
McGee, Raquel, *111*
McHugh, Laura, 28
McManus, Karen, 131
metacognition, 28, 63, *119*, 120
Meyer, Marissa, 138
Miller, Donalyn, 38
mini-unit, 48, 69–*70*, 72
modeling, 6, 9, 27, 29, 89, 96, 121
Moore, Alan, 134

Minerva, Laura, 45
Molloy, Joe, *39*
Myers, Walter Dean, 130

narrative, 46, 48, 51, 65–66, 72, 123
National Assessment of Educational Progress (NAEP), 7
National Council of Teachers of English (NCTE), *111*, 117; "Call to Action" (2018a), 36, 89, 92, 103, 105, 121; "Literacy Assessment" (2018b), 88, 89; "Statement on Classroom Libraries" (2017), 49; "Statement on Independent Reading" (2019), 4, 9, 97, 111; "The Students' Right to Read" (2018c), 52–53
National Endowment of the Arts (NEA), 122, 124; "To Read or Not to Read" (2007), 3, 4, 46, 71, 84, 90, 103, 113, 120; "U.S. Trends in Arts Attendance and Literary Reading" (2018), 4
National Writing Project, 117
NCTE. *See* National Council of Teachers of English
NEA. *See* National Endowment of the Arts
Nelson, Jandy, 133, 135
Neri, Gregory, 134
Ness, Patrick, 134
Niven, Jennifer, 129, 137
Noah, Trevor, 101, 136
nonfiction, 12, *21, 35,* 71–72, 87, 102
Notice and Note, 20, *21,* 86
Novak, B. J., 136

Oliver, Lauren, 129, 131
one-pager, 19–30, 32–35, 62, 65, *70,* 86, 90–91, *93,* 96, 99, 110, *119*
one-pager, rubric, 26–27
Orange, Tommy, 139

Palacio, R. J., 102
Paris, B. A., 131
Pelzer, Dave, 137
Perkins, Stephanie, 133

A Place Called School, 3, 32, 92
Poehler, Amy, 136
Postman, Neal, 108
Probst, Robert E., 20, 86
public sphere, 112

Quealy, Moira, *9,* 77
Quick, Matthew, 132
quick write, *27–28, 32, 34–36, 74, 119*
Quintero, Isabel, 139

racial responsiveness. *See* cultural responsiveness
Rae, Issa, 136
Ramilo, Gisele, *102,* 107
Raskin, Allison, 130
readers: struggling, *5,* 20, *27, 42,* 54, 63, 96, 109; readers, reluctant, 5–6, 12, 20, *42,* 49–52, 63,
Readicide, 6, *8,* 20, *21,* 86, 90–91, 115
reading: across contents, 71–72; daily, 4–*5,* 47, *93, 96*–97, 101, 109; rates, 50–51, 69, 109; tracking, 12
Reading in the Wild, 38
Reading Zone, 65, 85–86, 93, 105, 109, 113, 116
Rebele-Henry, Brynne, 138
Resnik, Lauren, 121
reflection, *22,* 28, 32, 38, 43–44, 51, 63, 97, 99, 100, *101,* 110
relationship skills, 96, 102, 103–104, 105
Renaissance, 85
Reynolds, Jason, 47, 110–111, 130, 139
Robinson, Phoebe, 136
Roe, Robin, 129
Rogan, Joe, 68
Rowell, Rainbow, *16, 17, 98,* 133
Rubin, Gretchen, 124
Russo, Meredith, 135

Sáenz, Benjamin Alire, *103,* 133, 135, 139
Salisbury, Graham, 131
Sanchez, Erika, 102, 129, 139

Sanchez, Reymundo, 102
Sapolsky, Robert, 101
SAT. *See* standardized testing
Satrapi, Marjane, 134
Schneider, Robyn, *113*, 132
Schumer, Amy, 136
Sebold, Alice, 128, 129
SEL. *See* social-emotional learning
self-awareness, 96–98
self-management, 96, 98–99
Shakespeare, William, 6, 138
Shamsie, Kamila, 138
Sheinmel, Alyssa B., 138
Sheppard, Dax, 68
Shusterman, Neal, 137
Silvera, Adam, 129, 135
Sims-Bishop, Rudine, *111*
Smith, Amber, 137
Smith, Andrew, *16*, 33, 132, 134
Smith, Michael, 113
social-emotional learning (SEL), 95–106
social awareness, 96, 101–103
socioeconomic responsiveness. *See* cultural responsiveness
special education, 61, 72
standardized testing, 11, 34, 83–84
STAR assessment, 85
Stein, Garth, 129
Steinbeck, John, 48
Stone, Nic, 139
"Student Story," *17, 49, 53, 98, 99, 101, 103, 104, 113, 119*
summer reading, 69–*70*, 88

Takano, Ichigo, *120*
"Teacher Tip," *9, 16, 102, 111, 118, 120*
Teaching as a Subversive Activity, 108
technology, how to deal with, 29, 51, 96–97, *99*

Telgemeier, Raina, 134
Tharp, Tim, 132
This Is Disciplinary Literacy, 71–72
Thomas, Angie, 114, 139
Thomas, Iain S., 130
Thompson, Craig, 134
time considerations, 46, 68–69, *70, 73–74,* 78; for discussion, *32*, 38, 92; for reading, 4–6, 46–48, 51, 84, 115–116, 121–122; for writing, 20, *27–28*, 29, 65–66
traditional. *See* teacher-centered
Twitter, 14, 16, 122

Udchik, Dave, 61

Vizzini, Ned, *119*, 132, 137

Walsh, Jennifer, 83
Waxler, Cary, 31
Westerfeld, Scott, 135
What Does It Mean to Be White?, 111–112
White, Kiersten, 138
whole-class study, 24, 33–34, 47–48, 58, 68–69, 71, 88, 107, 110–111, 115–116
Wilhelm, Jeffrey, 113, 117, 121
Wolitzer, Meg, *16*, 129, 131
Wolk, Steven, 104

Yang, Gene, 134
Yoon, Nicola, 129, 131, 133, 139
young adult literature (YAL), 6, 12, 13, *16, 17,* 21, *70, 77,* 88, 102, 110, *113, 120,* 127–139

Zoboi, Ibi, 139
Zomorodi, Manoush, 51

About the Authors

Stephanie Fleck teaches English and sponsors the literary magazine at Barrington High School in Barrington, Illinois. She has her MFA in creative writing from Augsburg University. She lives in the Chicago suburbs with her husband and daughter. You can follow her on Twitter @sweiss_teach.

Jolene Heinemann teaches English at Oak Park and River Forest High School in Oak Park, Illinois. She has her MA in English from Northeastern Illinois University. She lives in Chicago with her partner and their Flemish Giant rabbit. You can follow her much less active Twitter account @msheinemann.

Both Stephanie and Jolene are active on their shared Instagram account @choice_voice_teach.

www.ingramcontent.com/pod-product-compliance
Lightning Source LLC
Chambersburg PA
CBHW022014300426
44117CB00005B/187